# The Ethics and the Economics of Minimalist Government

*To Colleen Jo Healy*

# The Ethics and the Economics of Minimalist Government

Timothy P. Roth, Ph.D.

*The University of Texas at El Paso, USA*

**Edward Elgar**
Cheltenham, UK • Northampton, MA, USA

Published by
Edward Elgar Publishing Limited
Glensanda House
Montpellier Parade
Cheltenham
Glos GL50 1UA
UK

Edward Elgar Publishing Inc.
136 West Street
Suite 202
Northampton
Massachusetts 01060
USA

Reprinted 2003

A catalogue record for this book
is available from the British Library

**Library of Congress Cataloging-in-Publication Data**
Roth, Timothy P.
The ethics and the economics of minimalist government / Timothy P. Roth.
p. cm.
Includes bibliographical references and index.
1. Free enterprise—Moral and ethical aspects. 2. Economics—Moral and ethical aspects.
I. Title.

HB95 .R64 2002
320'.01—dc21

2002023260

ISBN 1 84064 676 4

Typeset by Manton Typesetters, Louth, Lincolnshire, UK.
Printed and bound in Great Britain by Biddles Ltd, *www.biddles.co.uk*

# Contents

# Preface

The economist's theory of the state is grounded in consequentialist, procedurally detached and intendedly value-free social welfare theory. Reduced to its essentials, the 'omniscient economist' deploys the first and second fundamental welfare theorems in the service of a 'benevolent despot'. The latter, in turn, is understood to be a 'bifurcated man'; narrowly self-interested in his market behaviour, but attentive, in his public persona, to a supraindividual 'public good' (Chapters 3, 4 and 5).

In their relentless pursuit of first-best Pareto-efficient outcomes economists seem to have ignored both an early admonition against 'piecemeal' welfare economics (Chapter 5), and a burgeoning literature which questions the empirical content and logical consistency of the neoclassical postulates which underlie their theory. As we shall see, once account is taken of some fundamental features of observable reality, the efficiency frontier and the social welfare function – whose ontological existence was questioned almost five decades ago – are indeterminate (Chapter 6). Granting this, the omniscient economist lacks the analytical tools by which, 'scientifically', to inform the policy deliberations of the benevolent despot who, 'himself', has no empirical counterpart. *Inter alia*, this admittedly convenient analytical fiction ignores the complexities of day-to-day, conflictual politics (Chapter 7). It follows that, while they proceed under the imprimatur of 'positive' or 'scientific' welfare economics, government interventions motivated by the fundamental welfare theorems must be regarded as *ad hoc*. Stated differently, neither 'market imperfections' nor presumed divergences between 'competitive' and 'ethical' equilibria can justify the implicit assumption that 'government can do better' (Chapters 4 and 5).

There is, however, a more fundamental problem. While it is a part of the corpus of intendedly value-free positive economics, social welfare theory is, in fact, a hybrid moral theory (Chapter 2). Because it is utilitarian, it is goal-based. Yet, because unattenuated property and exchange rights are instrumentally important to the achievement of first-best Paretian optima, social welfare theory incorporates elements of right-based moral theories. Difficulties arise because utilitarian social welfare theory cannot accommodate the moral force of rights. Indeed, there is a literature which endorses 'efficiency-enhancing' corruption (Chapter 5). It follows that, even if one granted its existence, the *path* to the efficiency frontier is not assured (Chapter 6). Moreover, because social welfare theory cannot accommodate any plausible understanding of justice (Chapter 2), in-period and intergenerational transfer programs cannot be justified by the theory.

The upshot is that social welfare theory is neither scientific nor an internally consistent moral theory. It follows, *pari passu*, that government interventions motivated by the theory can be neither scientifically nor morally justified. Considered in the context of conflictual or day-to-day politics, the implications are troubling. On the one hand, all manner of government programs and policies can be 'justified' by the theory. On the other hand, rent seekers have an incentive to appeal to the theory to justify both in-period and intergenerational transfers. In short, it seems clear that the size and scope of government has expanded beyond that which can be scientifically or morally justified (Chapter 10).

This book is part of the Kantian/Rawlsian contractarian enterprise. It rejects the consequentialist theory which, for most of the prior century, dominated the economist's approach to public policy appraisal. In its place it substitutes a prior ethical commitment to the moral equivalence of persons (Chapter 1). Given this commitment, certain corollaries follow. First, whereas social welfare theory is consequentialist, with the public good to be promoted understood to exist independently of the expression of individual values, I regard the autonomy, agency, independence, self-determination and dignity of morally equivalent persons as morally exigent. However, given the complexity and mutability of individual preference and value structures (Chapter 6), neither governments nor the economists who advise them can know, *a priori*, what individuals want. Second, whereas social welfare theory is procedurally detached, regards rights as merely instrumentally important, and cannot accommodate a theory of justice, the moral equivalence of persons implies a set of institutional imperatives. On the one hand, because rights must be given lexical priority, the greatest possible equal liberty or political participation must be promoted. Whereas utilitarian social welfare theory can provide only a contingent defense of constitutional democracy (Chapter 3), I assume, with Rawls, that a constitutional democracy can be arranged so as to satisfy this imperative (Rawls 1971, p. 222). On the other hand, justice as impartiality demands that, like the idealized rule of law, *all* government institutions respect the moral equivalence of persons (Chapter 8).

These institutional imperatives have implications for conflictual or day-to-day politics. *Inter alia*, the inherently discriminatory rent seeking which is characteristic of majoritarian democracy must be constitutionally constrained, legislators must pass just, in the sense of impartial, legislation, and the constitution must 'underwrite a fair opportunity to take part in and to influence the political process' (Rawls 1971, p. 224) (Chapter 8).

Because *individual* perceptions of the public good are determinative, a constitution informed by the moral equivalence of persons cannot determine *a priori* the precise size and scope of post-constitutional government (Chapter 10). What *can* be said is adumbrated, for a reasonably comprehensive array of public policy issues, in Chapter 9. A recurring theme is that impartiality- or generality-constrained conflictual politics would, in the limit, eliminate resource-wasting rent seeking, maximize equal political participation, and demand the non-discriminatory treatment of morally equivalent persons.

Finally, I wish to acknowledge my intellectual debt to Professor James M. Buchanan. I hope that my work comports with his vision of what economists should do.

# 1. A prior ethical commitment

## 1.1 INTRODUCTION

The protestations of many economists notwithstanding, economics is a moral science. The Adam Smith of *An Inquiry Into The Nature and Causes of The Wealth of Nations* was, after all, first the author of *The Theory of Moral Sentiments*. While the dominant image of Smith is that of an advocate of unfettered self-interest, in fact, the 'invisible hand' of *Wealth* was part and parcel of Smith's concern with how conscience is formed (Tribe 1999, p. 627). A recurring theme is therefore how the market and other institutions might be structured so as to cultivate the human desire for the sympathetic approval of others. Central to this project is the idea that 'the market', the law and other formal and informal institutions can assist in the development of the 'superior' and 'inferior' virtues.[1] In effect, the father of economics (Tribe 1999, p. 609) was, first and foremost, a moral philosopher.

The emergence of institutionless, intendedly value-free neoclassical economic theory meant, *inter alia*, that many economists either lost sight of, ignored, or rejected the moral foundation of economics. Indeed, the view became prevalent that value-judgments and normative issues generally do not fall under the purview of scientific, positive economics.

This view notwithstanding, it is relatively easy to show that social welfare theory – the theory which informs most economists' approach to public policy appraisal – is, in fact, a hybrid moral theory (§2.1). Because it is consequentialist, it is a part of the body of goal-based moral theories. And, because it regards unattenuated property and exchange rights as instrumentally important to the attainment of first-best Paretian optima, it is part of the corpus of right-based moral theories. Indeed, while social welfare theorists typically emphasize the efficacy of efficient or Pareto-optimal outcomes, many of the same theorists implicitly regard freedom as morally exigent in itself. Since rights determine the distribution of freedom it follows that, for these theorists, their consequentialist moral theory is inexorably bound up with right-based moral theories.

While these ideas are more fully explored in Chapter 4, immediate interest centers on the fact that, despite the commitment to institutionless, intendedly value-free analysis, economics has not, in fact, broken from its ethical moorings.

This idea animates the analysis deployed in this book. Central to the enterprise is the notion that economics is, and always has been, a moral science. Granting this, the ethical prior commitments upon which economic analysis is based should be made explicit.

## 1.2 THE MORAL EQUIVALENCE OF PERSONS

Writing in 1785, the great European moral philosopher, Immanuel Kant, argued that 'Whatever has reference to the general inclinations and wants of mankind has a market value'.[2] In contrast, 'that which constitutes the condition under which almost anything can be an end in itself, this has not merely a relative worth, that is, value, but an intrinsic worth, that is dignity' ([1785] 1988, p. 64). Granting this, the intrinsic worth or dignity of man – and of every rational creature – finds its basis in 'autonomy' (p. 65).

Given his autonomy,

> ...man and generally any rational being exists as an end in himself, not merely as a means to be arbitrarily used by this or that will, but in all his actions, whether they concern himself or other rational beings, must be always regarded at the same time as an end. All objects of the inclinations have only a conditional worth, for if the inclinations and the wants founded on them did not exist, then their object would have no value (pp. 56–57).

These passages make clear that, in contrast to utilitarian moral philosophy, Kant's ethics are not preference-based (Rawls [1989] 1999, pp. 502, 508 and 527). Moreover, the central importance of autonomy and the will is immediately apparent.

The core features of Kant's ethics can be appreciated once it is understood that he envisions man as thinking of himself 'as an intelligence endowed with a will, and consequently with causality'. But man also 'perceives himself as a phenomenon in the world of sense...and affirms that his causality is subject to external determination according to the laws of nature' ([1785] 1988, p. 90). For Kant, these two 'points of view' are not incompatible (pp. 84–85). Indeed, 'there is not the smallest contradiction in saying that a thing in appearance (belonging to the world of sense) is subject to certain laws, on which the very same as a thing or being in itself is independent....' (p. 90).

Reduced to its essentials, this is a view of man inhabiting a 'natural world of spatially and temporally extended objects that are causally connected' – but 'we have no reason to think that the knowable natural world is all there is' (O'Neill 1993, p. 176). Indeed, and on the contrary,

> ...we have and cannot do without a conception of ourselves as agents and as moral beings which makes sense only on the assumption that we have a free will...free will and natural causality are compatible, provided that human freedom – the capacity to act autonomously – is not taken to be an aspect of the natural world. Causality and freedom apply in separate domains; knowledge is restricted to the former and morality to the latter (O'Neill 1993, p. 176).

While Kant is clear that freedom of will must be 'presupposed' as a property of the will of all rational beings ([1785] 1988, pp. 79–80), he is equally clear that (p. 78)

> ...although freedom is not a property of the will depending on physical laws, yet it is not for that reason lawless; on the contrary it must be a causality acting according to immutable laws, but of a peculiar kind; otherwise a free will would be an absurdity.... What else then can freedom of the will be but autonomy, that is the property of the will to be a law to itself?

On this account, all moral conceptions 'have their seat and origins completely *a priori* in the reasons' (Kant [1785] 1988, pp. 38–39). For Kant, reason, as the governor of the will (p. 19), enables rational beings to act 'according to the conception of laws, that is according to principles, i.e., have a will. Since the deduction of actions from principles requires reason, the will is nothing but practical reason' (p. 40).

The 'immutable laws...of a peculiar kind', the 'principles' to which Kant refers, are 'legislated' by the free will of the rational, autonomous agent (Kant [1785] 1988, pp. 62–63). Autonomy of the will, then, is both the 'basis of the dignity of human and every rational nature' (p. 65), and the 'property of [the will] by which it is a law to itself (independently on any property of the objects of volition)' (p. 70). This, then, is what Kant means by the 'positive conception' of freedom: 'What else then can freedom of the will be but autonomy, that is the property of the will to be a law to itself?' (p. 78). Given this understanding 'we see that when we conceive ourselves as free we transfer ourselves into the world of understanding as members of it, and recognize the autonomy of the will with its consequence, morality' (p. 85). As John Rawls has emphasized:

> What is crucial for Kant's view is that the moral law must not be merely formal but have enough content to be...sufficient of itself to determine ends: pure reason is not merely finding the most effective way to realize given ends but it criticizes and selects among proposed ends. Its doing this is what Kant has in mind when he says that the moral law specifies a positive concept of freedom. We are free not only in the sense that we are able to act independently of our natural desires and needs, but also free in the sense that we have a principle regulative of both ends and means from which to act, a principle of autonomy appropriate to us as reasonable and rational beings ([1989] 1999, p. 525).

Importantly, given the 'two points of view', it is our consciousness of the moral law – as rational, autonomous beings – which 'discloses to us that we can stand fast against the totality of our natural desires; and this in turn discloses our capacity to act independently of the natural order' (Rawls [1989] 1999, p. 527).

And what is the 'moral law' that is legislated by a free will? Kant's answer is unambiguous:

> But the proposition: The will is in every action a law to itself, only expresses the principle, to act on no other maxim than that which can also have as an object itself as a universal law. Now this is precisely the formula of the categorical imperative and is the principle of morality, so that a free will and a will subject to moral laws are one and the same ([1785] 1988, p. 78).

While Kant formulates the categorical imperative in a number of ways, the idea which animates it is the conception of the moral equivalence of persons:

> The conception of free and equal persons as reasonable and rational is the basis of the construction: unless this conception and the powers of moral personality it includes – our humanity – are animated, as it were, in human beings, the moral law would have no basis in the world (Rawls [1989] 1999, p. 515).

## 1.3 THE CATEGORICAL IMPERATIVE

Kant distinguishes between hypothetical and categorical imperatives. Whereas the former represents 'the practical necessity of a possible action as means to something else that is willed (or at least which one might possibly will)', a categorical imperative 'would be that which represented an action as necessary of itself without reference to another end, that is, as objectively necessary' (Kant [1785] 1988, pp. 41–42).

With this as background, my interest centers on the categorical imperative (CI) or, more generally, the moral law. One formulation of the CI has already been invoked. The Formula of Universal Law says: 'Act only on that maxim whereby thou canst at the same time will that it should become a universal law' (Kant [1785] 1988, p. 49). But the formulation which 'has had the greatest cultural impact' (O'Neill 1993, p. 178) is the Formula of the End in Itself: 'So act as to treat humanity, whether in thine own person or in that of any other, in every case as an end withal, never as a means only' (Kant [1785] 1988, p. 58).

The Formula of the End in Itself demands, then, that we respect the autonomy, agency, independence, self-determination and dignity of morally equivalent persons. On this account, it is not persons' 'utility' or 'happiness' that is intrinsically valuable. On the one hand, morality cannot be grounded in 'private happiness' since 'the springs it provides for morality…put the motives to virtue and to vice in the same class, and only teach us to make a better calculation, the specific difference between virtue and vice being entirely extinguished' (Kant [1785] 1988, p. 72).[3] On the other hand, 'a man cannot form any definite and certain conception of the sum of satisfaction of all (his inclinations) which is called happiness' (pp. 23–24).[4] In effect, grounding morality on utility or happiness opens the door to all manner of casuistries and, in any case, would implicate an essentially indeterminate evaluative standard. These considerations underscore the contrast between what John Rawls characterizes as Kant's CI procedure and utilitarianism ([1989] 1999, pp. 507–508). This contrast informs much of the discussion in later chapters.

Given that persons are morally equivalent, each is entitled to equal or impartial consideration. Each person has a duty to respect the intrinsic worth of others (and of himself); a duty which 'does not rest at all on feelings, impulses or inclinations, but solely on the relation of rational beings to one another' (Kant [1785] 1988, p. 63). Thus, whereas utilitarianism is consequentialist, with the maximization of utility as the ultimate desideratum or 'good', the CI – or moral law – is procedural or contractarian:

> Rather than starting from a conception of the good given independently of the right, we start with a conception of the right – of the moral law – given by pure (as opposed to empirical) practical reason. We then specify in the light of this conception what ends are permissible and what social arrangements are right and just (Rawls [1989] 1999, p. 509).

The specification of 'right and just' social arrangements implicates the question of institutional design. On Kant's account, persons' free will renders possible a 'kingdom of ends'; an idea which, while 'certainly only an ideal' contemplates a social contract among persons who both legislate and are subject to universalizable laws (Kant [1785] 1988, pp. 62–63). Because, however, persons are morally equivalent, freedom of action is restricted (p. 57): What is legislated must be 'respect for others' like status as legislators' (O'Neill 1993, p. 179).[5] The demand for equal consideration, in turn, 'gives rise at the social level to a "natural duty of justice"': 'We have a duty to promote just institutions, a duty not derived from consent or mutual advantage, but simply owed to persons as such' (Kymlicka 1993, p. 191).

## 1.4 HOBBESIAN VERSUS KANTIAN CONTRACTARIANISM

The duty to promote just institutions requires that a procedure exists to determine the meaning of justice. The social contract device is one such procedure. Two contemporary contractarian theories deploy the device, and both accept the view that persons are, by nature, equals. Because Hobbesian contractarianism regards justice as mutual advantage it 'stresses a natural equality of physical power, which makes it mutually advantageous for people to accept conventions that recognize and protect each other's interests and possessions' (Kymlicka 1993, p. 188).

While the view of justice as mutual advantage is encumbered by a number of empirical and logical difficulties (§ 2.21 and Roth 1999, pp. 65–67), the core problem is that it 'does not view individuals as having any inherent moral rights or status' (Kymlicka 1993, p. 189). In effect, nothing in the mutual advantage approach contemplates moral claims which are prior to the pursuit of mutual advantage.

In sharp contrast, the theory of justice as impartiality is grounded in Kant's categorical imperative. Central to this project is the idea of a social contract which embodies a basic principle of impartial deliberation (Kymlicka 1993, p. 191). The presumption is that, whereas man perceives himself from 'two points of view' – as a rational person possessed of free will and, at the same time, as a phenomenon in the world of sense and therefore subject to the laws of nature[6] – moral legislation is to be agreed to under conditions which characterize men as free and equal rational beings:

> Kant held, I believe, that a person is acting autonomously when the principles of his action are chosen…as a free and rational being. The principles he acts upon are not adopted because of his social position or natural endowments… To act on such principles is to act heteronomously (Rawls 1971, p. 252).[7]

If, in other words, rational persons are to act morally – to choose principles of justice consistent with the CI – each must be deprived of some information. According to this, impartial deliberation requires that 'The principles of…actions do not depend upon social or natural contingencies, nor reflect the bias of the particulars of [negotiators'] plan[s] of life or the aspirations that motivate them' (Rawls 1971, p. 252).

What is envisioned, then, is an 'original position' characterized by a 'veil of ignorance' (Rawls 1971, pp. 136–142).[8]

## 1.5 THE ORIGINAL POSITION AND THE VEIL OF IGNORANCE

Given that all persons are morally equivalent, the choice among principles of justice requires that those principles not be adopted heteronomously; that they not be affected by persons' social positions, natural endowments, life plans or preference structures. Granting this, the original position must be characterized by both informational deprivation and informational symmetry:

> The principles of justice are chosen behind a veil of ignorance. This ensures that no one is advantaged or disadvantaged in the choice of principles by the outcome of natural chance or the contingency of social circumstances. Since all are similarly situated and no one is able to design principles in favor of his particular condition, the principles of justice are the result of a fair agreement or bargain ...this initial situation is fair between individuals as moral persons, that is, as rational beings with their own ends and capable, I shall assume, of a sense of justice ... thus the fundamental agreements reached in it are fair. This explains the propriety of the name 'justice as fairness' (Rawls 1971, p. 12).

The essential ideas are that, given the moral equivalence of persons, moral judgements 'are, or should be, impartial', and 'Justice as fairness provides what we want. An impartial judgment...is one rendered in accordance with the principles which would be chosen in the original position' (Rawls 1971, p. 190).[9] These considerations – and others – lead Rawls to assert that 'The original position may be viewed...as a procedural interpretation of Kant's conception of autonomy and the categorical imperative' (Rawls 1971, p. 256).[10] On this account, then, 'The notion of the veil of ignorance is implicit...in Kant's ethics' (Rawls 1971, pp. 140–141).

## 1.6 THE MORAL EQUIVALENCE OF PERSONS, AGAIN

The idea which motivates the demand for impartial consideration – and, *pari passu*, the notion that contracting in the original position must proceed behind a veil of ignorance – is the moral equivalence of persons. That said, it is important to understand that the 'contract device' cannot justify this basic moral judgment; it presupposes it. While the veil of ignorance construct 'attempts to render vivid the idea that other people matter in and of themselves, not simply as a component of our own good', the contract device 'is simply an expression of prior moral commitments' (Kymlicka 1993, p. 194). Nevertheless, while the Kantian/Rawlsian contract device cannot justify the basic moral judgement that persons are morally equivalent, it does serve some useful purposes:

> It can render our judgments more determinate (contractual agreements must be explicitly and publicly formulated), render them more vivid (the veil of ignorance is a vivid way of expressing the moral requirement of putting ourselves in other people's shoes), and can dramatize our commitment to them (the veil of ignorance dramatizes the claim that we would accept a certain principle however it affected us). In these and other ways, the contract device illuminates the basic ideas of morality as impartiality, even if it cannot help defend those ideas (Kymlicka 1993, p. 193).

## 1.7 THE POLITICAL IMPLICATIONS OF THE CATEGORICAL IMPERATIVE

In Chapters 7 and 8 emphasis is placed on the distinction between constitutional and conflictual or day-to-day politics. The former contemplates determination – ideally in an original position in which decisions are affected behind a veil of ignorance – of the rules-of-the-game for, and the constraints on, conflictual politics. For the moment, my interest centers on the constitutional stage.

As has been emphasized, the moral equivalence of persons demands that their autonomy, agency, independence, self-determination and dignity be respected. This idea, drawn from moral philosophy, has an analog in political philosophy. The principle of equal participation

> ...requires that all citizens are to have an equal right to take part in, and to determine the outcome of, the constitutional process that establishes the laws with which they are to comply. Justice as fairness begins with the idea that where common principles are necessary and to everyone's advantage, they are to be worked out from the viewpoint of a suitably defined initial situation of equality in which each person is fairly represented. The principle of participation transfers this notion from the original position to the constitution as the highest-order system of social rules for making rules (Rawls 1971, pp. 221–222).

The principle of equal participation implies an institutional – in this case, constitutional – imperative: *inter alia*, 'firm constitutional protections must be provided for certain liberties, particularly freedom of speech and assembly, and liberty to form political associations' (Rawls 1971, pp. 222–223). In short, the principle of equal participation – or, what is the same thing, of equal liberty (p. 221) – contemplates a constitutional democracy (Rawls 1971, pp. 222 and 225). In Kantian terms, rational persons are, in the kingdom of ends, both legislators and subject to their, ideally, universalizable laws. When – in the original position and behind the veil of ignorance – they choose the constitutional rules of the conflictual politics game they will take account of the moral equivalence of persons: 'We...know that under favourable conditions, a realm of ends is some form of constitutional democracy' (Rawls [1989] 1999, p. 526).[11]

A constitutional democracy can, in principle, be arranged so as to satisfy the principle of equal participation (Rawls 1971, pp. 222). To do so requires that the constitution satisfy the requirements of equal liberty. But it also requires that the constitution 'be framed so that of all the feasible just arrangements, it is the one more likely than any other to result in a just and effective system of legislation' (Rawls 1971, p. 221). In short, given the moral equivalence of persons, the constitution must give lexical priority to rights. But it must also provide rules of the conflictual politics game which are consonant with the emergence of just – in the sense of impartial – legislation (§§ 8.2 and 9.8).

It is clear, then, that an ethical prior commitment to the moral equivalence of persons has implications both for constitutional and for conflictual politics. Granting this, the balance of this book provides both an adumbration of the implications for institutional design and government policy of the moral imperative to treat persons as moral equals, and a critical appraisal of the theory which economists standardly deploy to evaluate government action.

## 1.8 OVERVIEW AND PLAN OF THE BOOK

As the discussion in Chapter 1 makes clear, this book stands squarely in the Kantian/Rawlsian social contract tradition. The contrasts between this contractarian project and consequentialism is the focus of Chapter 2. *Inter alia*, the analysis suggests that consequentialism is reconcilable neither with the moral force of rights nor with justice regarded as rights protection, mutual advantage or impartiality. It is shown, moreover, that the understanding of justice which is implicit in social welfare theory ignores how distributive shares come about, and endorses the notion that structurally identical distributions are equally just.

The consequentialist approach to government is the focus of Chapter 3. Emphasis is placed on utilitarianism, the theory of the good which is most often employed to fill out the larger consequentialist framework. It is recognized that utilitarianism is, first and foremost, a standard for the appraisal of public action. Regardless of the form in which it is expressed, the imperative is to promote 'good consequences'. In the context of constitutional and conflictual or day-to-day politics, this translates to an imperative to promote a supraindividual 'public good'; a good which is understood to exist independently of the expression of individual values. This idea, in turn, finds expression in a social preference or welfare function.

In sharp contrast to the contractarian's approach to government, the utilitarian cannot respect the moral force of rights, cannot defend the institutions which are instrumentally important to promotion of the public good and, most important, cannot overcome the ontological objection to his organic conception of the public good. It follows that utilitarian social welfare theory is an inappropriate standard for public policy appraisal.

The social welfare theory which has for more than five decades shaped the economist's theory of the state is grounded in consequentialist theory. While intendedly value-free and deliberately institutionless, it is, in fact, a hybrid moral theory. Because it assigns an instrumental role to unattenuated property and exchange rights social welfare theory incorporates elements of right-based moral theories. And, because it contemplates a duty to promote 'good consequences' – in particular, the constrained maximization of 'social welfare' – it incorporates elements of goal-based moral theories. Emphasis is placed upon the specification of an efficiency or welfare frontier and a social welfare function. Achievement of points on the efficiency frontier is predicated – given a frictionless decision environment and unattenuated property and exchange rights – upon satisfaction of three well known 'welfare conditions' or marginal equivalences. These 'positive' conditions find normative expression in the efficiency standard; in the admonition that, when one or more of the marginal equivalences is not satisfied, public policy should be employed to correct the 'market failure'. On this logic, the first fundamental welfare theorem suggests that 'government intervention' may be required to achieve 'competitive equilibria', or points on the efficiency frontier. For its part, the second fundamental welfare theorem suggests that, given a social welfare function, lump-sum taxes and bounties may be employed to reconcile competitive and ethical equilibria. Chapter 4 is given over to an explication and preliminary critique of this received theory.

Chapter 5 explores some of the – apparently – unintended consequences of reliance on the received social welfare theory. On the one hand, while neoclassical economists tend to regard rights as instrumentally and, or, intrinsically valuable, a literature has grown up which regards corruption as potentially 'efficiency enhancing'. This particular casuistry is troublesome in its own right. It is anomalous in the sense that it cannot plausibly be reconciled with neoclassical economists' commitment to 'the market mechanism'; a mechanism which relies importantly upon the intervention of trust. On the other hand, the same neoclassical commitment to the efficacy of 'the market' is hardly congruent with the propensity to invoke the first fundamental welfare theorem to rationalize all manner of government interventions. These interventions, in turn, have been congenial to opportunistic exploitation; to the emergence of political rent seeking and the asymmetric treatment both of consumers and producers. Finally, invocations of the second fundamental welfare theorem have resulted in the proliferation of in-period and intergenerational transfer programs uninformed by a defensible theory of justice.

Chapter 6 addresses the implications for social welfare theory of the explicit incorporation of some fundamental features of observable reality. A relaxation of the underlying neoclassical behavioral and technological postulates, of the zero transaction cost convention, and of the associated rights construal renders the efficiency frontier indeterminate. Yet, even if the existence of the frontier were granted, the fact that the moral force of rights cannot be accommodated jeopardizes the path to first-best Paretian optima. The same is true of the zero transaction cost assumption; an analytical convenience which is, unintendedly, but logically, congenial to the formation of 'efficiency-reducing' coalitions. Finally, both the impossibility of in-period and intertemporal interpersonal utility comparisons and the impossibility of the Paretian liberal militate against the specification of a social welfare function. Even more fundamentally, because it implies an organic existence independent of the expression of individual values, it is possible to question the notion of 'social preference' (Chapter 3). These – and other – considerations suggest that public policy initiatives informed by the two fundamental welfare theorems must be regarded as *ad hoc*.

An alternative to consequentialist social welfare theory, contractarianism, is the subject of Chapter 7. Of immediate interest is the contractarian approach to government. As the logic developed in Chapter 1 suggests, a defining characteristic of the Kantian/Rawlsian contractarian enterprise is a prior commitment to the moral equivalence of persons. Central to the project – and to the concomitant approach to government – is the lexical priority of rights and respect for their correlative duties, recognition of the inability to prespecify endogenous and complex 'final ends and desires', and a procedural imperative to promote just or impartial institutions. Granting all of this, day-to-day or conflictual politics must be constrained by a constitution which demands both the greatest possible equal liberty or political participation, and the impartial treatment of morally equivalent persons. Impartiality or generality requires, in turn, that all political actions 'apply to all persons independently of membership in a dominant coalition or an effective interest group'. Given the *ad hoc* deployment of the fundamental welfare theorems and the difficulties which inhere in conflictual politics – in particular, rent seeking and majoritarian cycling – these principles would, ideally, be codified in a set of constitutional constraints on political action. Moreover, because trust is a *sine qua non* for the legitimacy of government, and impartial treatment is congenial to the emergence of trust, the constitutional rules within which conflictual politics unfold must reflect both the greatest possible equal liberty or political participation and the impartiality or generality norm.

The constitutional rules of the conflictual politics 'game' are the subject of Chapter 8. Central to this discussion is the distinction between 'economic' and 'political' efficiency. Whereas the former contemplates the efficiency standard to which the received social welfare theory gives rise, the latter focuses evaluative attention on the efficacy of differing institutions 'in reducing or eliminating the incentive for [conflictual politics'] participants to invest resources in rent seeking aimed to secure discriminatory advantage through majoritarian exploitation'. In effect, whereas economic efficiency concentrates on 'getting the prices right', the political efficiency standard regards 'getting the institutions right' as the desideratum. The imperative to 'get the institutions right' demands, in turn, that the principles which inform the idealized rule of law – its external and internal morality – apply to *all* of the institutions of post-constitutional or conflictual politics.

The balance of Chapter 8 concentrates on an explication of the need to engage in constitutional discourse and on the incentive to agree on a constitution informed by Kantian/Rawlsian principles.

Chapter 9, 'Playing by the generality rule', compares the observable outcomes of ordinary, conflictual – and, therefore, discriminatory – politics with what might be achieved under a constitutional regime which promotes the greatest possible equal political participation, and demands that morally equivalent persons be impartially treated. Attention centers on observed discriminatory policies falling under such rubrics as general taxation, government outlays, government credit programs, government borrowing, redistribution, social insurance, and interventions in internal and external markets. The essential idea is that the costs of discriminatory policies – including the resources expended in rent seeking activities and the erosion of trust in government – can be reduced by appeal to policies constrained by the greatest possible equal political participation and an impartiality or generality principle.

Finally, the argument suggests that the legislative process should itself be constrained by the requirement that its product, the body of statutory law, be just or impartial. *Inter alia*, laws – and the legislative process itself – should be general, transparent, prospective, and stable. Absent a commitment to such principles the legislative process is congenial, given bounded rationality and all that it implies, to the emergence of opportunistic behavior; to deliberate obfuscation, the surreptitious conference of discriminatory benefits, and the in-period and intergenerational shifting of costs. That all of this is part of the warp and woof of unconstrained conflictual politics is itself an argument for a constitutional impartiality or generality constraint. Nothing less than trust in, and the legitimacy of, government is at stake.

The final chapter, 'Generality and minimalist government', emphasizes that institutionalization of Kantian/Rawlsian principles implies neither an 'optimal' size or scope of government. These issues are resolved at the post-constitutional stage, given equally weighted, individual assessments of the public good. What is, however, clear is that a rejection of the economists' romanticized view of politics, when accompanied by appropriate constitutional constraints, would reduce rent seeking and the concomitant growth of government. It is in this sense that an institutional regime grounded in the moral equivalence of persons and relieved of the 'duty to promote good consequences' would minimize both the size and the intrusiveness of government.

## NOTES

1. J.Z. Muller's *Adam Smith in His Time and Ours* (1993) provides an adumbration of these and related ideas. Myerson (1999) notes that 'the term economics was first used by philosophers of ancient Greece who were interested in studying all the institutions of civilized society and did not develop an academic specialization in the study of markets alone'. On this logic he concludes that 'it was natural then for economics to develop as a special branch of moral philosophy....' (p. 1068). For more on the so-called 'Adam Smith problem', see Blaug (2001, p. 158)
2. The discussion in Chapter 1 is animated by Immanuel Kant's 1785 work, *Fundamental Principles of the Metaphysic of Morals*. While Kant was a prolific author, the focus on this book is motivated, in part, by the observation that '... Kant's *Groundwork of the Metaphysic of Morals* is one of the small books which are truly great: it has exercised on human thought an influence almost ludicrously disproportionate to its size. In moral philosophy it ranks with the *Republic* of Plato and the *Ethics* of Aristotle ... (Paton, 1964, p. 8).
3. More generally, Kant is clear that 'Empirical principles are incapable of serving as a foundation for moral laws' ([1785] 1988, p. 71). The essential idea is that 'all moral conceptions have their seat and origin completely *a priori* in the reason...they cannot be obtained by abstraction from any empirical, and therefore merely contingent knowledge....' ([1785] 1988, pp. 38–39). See also Paton (1964, p. 51).
4. See also Kant ([1785] 1988, pp. 19, 45, 52 and 74). The essential point is that 'although every man wishes to attain [happiness], yet he never can say definitely and consistently what it is that he really wishes and wills' (p. 45). For more on this, see Rawls ([1989], 1999 p. 519).
5. See also Rawls ([1989] 1999, p. 524).
6. The key idea is that Kant envisions a dual view of man: 'we are both phenomenal (natural, causally determined) beings and noumenal (non-natural, self-determining) beings' (O'Neill 1993, p. 180).
7. See also Kant ([1785] 1988, pp. 62 and 70–75).
8. See also Rawls ([1989] 1999, p. 516).
9. See also Kymlicka (1993, p. 192).
10. Ronald Dworkin appears to agree with this procedural interpretation of the original position: 'The original position is...a schematic representation of a particular mental process of at least some, and perhaps most, human beings ...' (1978, p. 158).
11. See also Rawls (1996, pp. XVIII and XX). When a society is characterized by 'reasonable pluralism' in the sense that individuals 'affirm different and opposing though reasonable' comprehensive religious, philosophical or moral doctrines, social cooperation requires a 'thick rather than a thin' veil of ignorance. In effect, parties in the original position are deprived, *inter alia*, of knowledge of the comprehensive doctrines of those they represent (Rawls 1996, pp. 24–25).

# 2. Ends vs. means: consequentialism vs. contractarianism

## 2.1 CONSEQUENTIALISM AND THE MORAL FORCE OF RIGHTS

Ethical theories are typically characterized as theories of the right or theories of the good (Goodin 1993, p. 241). As we have seen, contractarians do not start with a concept of the good, given independently of the right. In particular, Kantian/Rawlsian contractarians begin with a conception of the right, the moral equivalence of persons. Given this, they specify permissible ends and the constitutions which are right and just.

In sharp contrast, consequentialists begin with a theory of the good and insist that that good ought to be promoted (Pettit 1993, p. 231). It is in this spirit that utilitarianism – the theory of the good which is most standardly employed to fill out the consequentialist framework – insists that the right action is that which maximizes utility summed across all those affected by the action.

While much can be said about this, immediate interest centers on an elementary idea: Whether expressed in hedonistic, preference or welfare form (§ 3.1), utilitarianism cannot respect the moral force of rights.

To see this, consider first that there is a taxonomy of rights: While they may be active, conveying a right to do things, they may also be passive, contemplating rights to have things done for or to one. More broadly, the differences among them subsume rights as claims, as powers, as liberties and as immunities. However, the 'dominant meaning may well be "claim", and in this, which is also its narrowest sense, it is the correlative of "duty"' (Almond 1993, p. 262).[1] At issue, then, is whether a right carries with it the moral obligation or duty to respect it. Of particular interest is whether consequentialist-utilitarian social welfare theory – the theory standardly deployed by economists in public policy appraisal – can accommodate the moral force of rights.

As we shall see (Chapter 4), social welfare theory assigns an instrumental role to unattenuated property and exchange rights. In the situation envisioned, such rights are instrumental to the achievement of first-best Paretian or 'efficient' outcomes. Indeed, some social welfare theorists regard 'freedom' – and, *pari passu*, the rights which determine its distribution – as morally exigent in itself. The essential point, however, is that, given their particular rights construal, social welfare theorists make the implicit assumption that instrumentally important and/or intrinsically valuable rights will be respected. In effect, then, utilitarian –and, therefore, consequentialist – social welfare theory embodies elements of right- and goal-based moral theories.[2] The problem is that right- and goal-based moral theories are irreconcilable:

> ...utilitarian arguments for institutional design (the arguments that utilitarians might use in favor of establishing or maintaining certain legal rights) do not logically or morally exclude direct utilitarian arguments concerning the exercise of, or interference with such rights. As a consequence, evaluation of conduct from a utilitarian standpoint is dominated by direct utilitarian arguments and therefore ignores the moral force of justified legal rights (Lyons 1982, p. 113).

Roughly paraphrased, the problem is that, in the utilitarian framework, utility considerations trump rights: '[Rights] appear to be unacceptable to utilitarians since they impede the unfettered pursuit of the social good' (Almond 1993, p. 266). Significantly, the Nobel laureate social welfare/social choice theorist Amartya Sen has emphasized that 'no direct and basic importance is attached in the utilitarian framework to rights and liberties in the evaluation of states of affairs' (1995, p. 13). That said, he asserts that 'The need to incorporate some "minimal liberties" on a priority basis can be incorporated in social choice formulations' (1995, p. 13). Sen's project is motivated by his rejection of the notion of preference-independent, consequence-detached rights. In rejecting the libertarian view of rights as absolute side constraints on action, he argues that 'perhaps the central question that is raised is the plausibility of making people's putative rights, in general, so dissociated from the effects of exercising them' (p. 14).[3] On the logic that rights cannot be consequence-detached Sen argues that consequential analysis can be employed in 'inverse form' to determine which rights to protect. While his idea is to embed rights protections in consequences or 'states of affairs', the difficulty is that rights – and duties – 'have a normative life of their own, with implications that are neither reducible to, nor traceable by, direct consideration of utility' (Lyons 1982, p. 133).[4] In effect, desired consequences cannot be employed to determine which rights to protect. Whether the rights which one seeks to protect are intrinsically valuable or merely instrumental, they cannot be derived from desired consequences. This objection applies with equal force to what has been styled rule-utilitarianism. While it can be expressed in preference or welfare form (§ 3.1), rule-utilitarianism 'limits the application of the standard of utility to rules or social institutions and requires compliance with rules that are certified as having the requisite utilitarian justification' (Lyons 1982, p. 128).

Like Sen's consequentialist-procedural approach (§ 2.23), rule-utilitarianism may appear to resolve the problem of respecting rights. There is, however, a logical problem: If a utilitarian believes that certain rules are justified on utilitarian grounds, he does not contradict himself 'by supposing that direct utilitarian arguments for deviating from the rules may be entertained' (Lyons 1982, p. 129). Reduced to its essentials, the rule-utilitarian 'cannot regard the morally defensible rights under utilitarian institutions as having moral force' (ibid.).[5]

To sum up, utilitarianism, the theory of the good which most commonly fills out the consequentialist framework, is irreconcilable with the moral force of rights. Because social welfare theory is utilitarian it follows that the rights which the theory regards as instrumentally important and/or intrinsically valuable need not be respected: Utility considerations can always trump rights. It follows that, even if one grants its existence, the path to the social welfare theoretic efficiency or welfare frontier is not assured (§ 6.4). This, along with an explicit accounting of some fundamental features of observable reality, calls into question the only evaluative standard to which social welfare theory gives rise (§ 6.3).

The implications of all of this for public policy appraisal will be explored in later chapters. For the moment it is sufficient to note one additional conundrum. Whereas utilitarianism and, *pari passu*, social welfare theory are not reconcilable with the moral force of rights and their correlative duties, *respect* for rights generates a different, methodological problem: Respecting minimal liberty appears, under plausible conditions, to rule out the possibility of any social choice. All that is required for this indeterminancy to emerge is that persons care about others' consumption patterns – and that 'privacy' rights be respected. As we shall see (§ 6.5), the 'impossibility of the Paretian liberal' (Sen 1995, p. 13) calls into question the efficacy of a social welfare function as an interest-aggregation decision mechanism. In effect, whereas the inability to accommodate the moral force of instrumentally important rights impedes the path to 'competitive equilibria', respect for privacy rights militates against the determination of 'ethical equilibria' (Chapter 6). Were nothing else to be said, the irreconcilability of rights and utilitarianism suggest that consequentialist social welfare theory is an inappropriate standard for public policy appraisal. Given that 'most students of public policy prefer the idiom of utilitarian analysis' (Waldron 1995, p. 581), and given that 'Utilitarianism of whatever stripe is, first and foremost, a standard for judging public action' (Goodin 1993, p. 245), this is, at best, problematic. What is in any case clear is that social welfare theorists must make a choice:

> Either they shall consider efficiency the sole fundamental basis for normative appraisal...or they must accept the idea that there are other values to be served

beyond economic efficiency, in which case they must entertain the possibility of rights and obligations that are independent of social recognition and enforcement; rights and obligations that justified legal institutions ought to respect (Lyons 1982, p. 128).

In effect, while social welfare theorists employ a hybrid moral theory, they cannot legitimately do so. Either they must argue that the rights which they regard as important are morally exigent in themselves and reject the only evaluative standard to which their theory gives rise (Pareto optimality or efficiency), or they must embrace the efficiency standard and deny the moral force of rights.

## 2.2 CONSEQUENTIALISM AND OTHER DIMENSIONS OF MORAL EVALUATION

It is clear that, as utilitarians, social welfare theorists cannot give lexical priority to rights. While the 'special force of rights' may be understood in one of three ways, the understanding which has basic relevance to consequentialist social welfare theory is that 'a right is nothing but a particularly important interest. While it is assigned a greater weight than ordinary interests, it can, in principle, be outweighed' (Waldron 1995, p. 15). If one grants that 'rights have priority over conditions like utility or desert because they reflect the conditions under which it becomes possible for an agent to recognize and act on considerations like utility and desert' (Waldron 1995, p. 19), this poses a dilemma for social welfare theorists. Finally, if one regards justice as respect for rights (Nozick 1974, pp. 150–153), this too poses a dilemma for social welfare theorists interested in making 'social judgments'. Given the inability of the theory to accommodate the moral force of rights, social welfare theory cannot, *mutatis mutandis*, regard justice as respect for rights.[6]

If the accommodation of rights poses an intractable problem for utilitarian social welfare theory, so too does justice. On the one hand, the theory cannot regard justice as respect for rights. On the other hand, social welfare theory does not deploy an explicit definition of justice. Consider, for example, that the theory suggests that initial resource endowments – which are themselves unexplained – are important determinants, given relative prices and unattenuated property and exchange rights, of the point on the efficiency frontier to which a perfectly competitive system is impelled. The theory is, however, silent about the justice – however defined – both of the 'competitive equilibrium' to which the system gravitates, and of the initial endowments.[7]

While social welfare theory does not invoke an explicit understanding of justice, it does distinguish between competitive and ethical equilibria (§§ 4.3 and 4.4). Each point on the efficiency frontier is Pareto optimal or efficient, and each represents a potential competitive equilibrium. At a cross-section of time, the competitive equilibrium is determinate, given certain 'simplifying assumptions'.[8] Indeed, the essence of the first fundamental welfare theorem is that a perfectly competitive system will automatically move to a unique, first-best Pareto-optimal competitive equilibrium (Novshek and Sonnenschein 1987; Duffie and Sonnenschein 1989). Emphasis is placed, however, on the notion that the competitive equilibrium to which the system is impelled may or may not be the 'socially desired' or ethical equilibrium. Reduced to its essentials, the latter is determined at a cross-section of time by the tangency of a social indifference curve and the efficiency frontier.[9]

Granting all of this, the second fundamental welfare theorem indicates that, no matter to which point on the efficiency frontier a perfectly competitive economy is automatically impelled, a different Pareto-efficient but 'socially desired' allocation can be realized by appeal to lump-sum taxes and bounties (Graaff 1957, pp. 75–83).

Putting aside the empirical, logical and other difficulties which attend this formulation (Chapter 6), the immediate question is: Does the ethical equilibrium contemplated by the theory subsume any understanding of justice?

First, there is an important sense in which the question begs an even more fundamental question: Can a social welfare function be deployed to determine an ethical equilibrium? Stated differently, the question is whether the notional social welfare function has an operational counterpart. As we have seen, under plausible conditions the impossibility of the Paretian liberal militates against the emergence of any social choice. Moreover, as is well known, Arrow's Possibility Result establishes that, if interpersonal utility comparisons are ruled out, there is no possible method of aggregating individual rankings of social alternatives which meets five apparently innocuous criteria (Arrow 1951, pp. 24–31). Further, it is possible to raise a fundamental, ontological problem. It is possible, in short, to reject not only the transitivity of social preference, but the idea of social preference itself (§ 3.2). While these and other fundamental problems are the subject of Chapters 3 and 6, the essential idea is that the social welfare function does not have an operational counterpart. Granting this, the 'ethical equilibrium' is indeterminate.

Suppose for the moment, however, that a single-valued, consistently-ordered utilitarian social welfare function can be deployed. Granting this, it is important to recall that the function may be understood to be an interest-aggregation mechanism which defines the optimal social outcome as the maximization of the sum of individual utilities. It is in this sense that the social welfare function is proffered as a mechanism for deciding among end states. Yet, because the function is utilitarian, it presupposes the normative judgment that the desideratum, the standard of outcome evaluation, is that the best state is that which maximizes aggregate utility or 'welfare'. That said, it is clear that preference satisfaction may not be an adequate conception of individual and, *pari passu*, 'social' well being. *Inter alia*, preferences may be based on false, idiosyncratic, highly contestable or malign beliefs. Moreover, as Hausman and McPherson have emphasized, there may be circumstances in which preferences should have to be 'laundered' before becoming suitable objects to be accorded moral weight (1993, p. 714). These considerations suggest that, even if one were to suppose that the notional social welfare function has an operational counterpart, the 'moral weight' of the ethical equilibrium could be called into question.

With all of this as background, the question remains: Does consequentialist social welfare theory accommodate any understanding of justice? Reduced to its essentials, justice – whether of the distributive or the commutative type – is a procedural notion (Scruton 1994, p. 425). It is a concept which, on this understanding, 'makes sense only when applied to the dealings between people' (pp. 424–425).

The two theories of procedural justice which have been characterized as the 'leading contenders' (Barry 1989, p. XIII) have already been encountered (§ 1.4). The first regards justice as mutual advantage, while the second regards justice as impartiality. The question at issue, then, is this: Can consequentialist social welfare theory accommodate either of these understandings of justice?[10]

## 2.21 Justice as Mutual Advantage

As one of two contemporary contractarian or social contract theories, the theory of justice as mutual advantage accepts the view that persons are, by nature, equals. However, whereas Kantian justice as impartiality stresses the moral equivalence of persons, justice as mutual advantage stresses a 'natural equality of physical power, which makes it mutually advantageous for people to accept conventions that recognize and protect each other's interests and possessions' (Kymlicka 1993, p. 188).

Central to the mutual advantage project is the notion that, whereas there is nothing inherently right or wrong about the goals which persons pursue, or the means adopted to pursue them, it is mutually advantageous for persons to adopt conventions against harming each other (Kymlicka 1993, p. 189). On this account, the adopted conventions constitute the 'social contract' which, in turn, provides a moral code; a code which is 'generated as a rational constraint from the non-moral premises of rational choice' (Gauthier 1986, p. 4). Significantly, the obligation to respect the adopted conventions is grounded in the idea that bargaining proceeds 'among expected utility maximizers with common knowledge of everyone's capabilities, endowments, and preferences' (Hausman and McPherson 1996, p. 158). This rich informational base, in turn, is regarded as a bargaining constraint: A rational agent is presumed never to agree to accept less than he could get in the absence of agreement.[11]

While the bargaining constraint is reminiscent of the logic employed by social welfare theorists in deriving contract curves, and *mutatis mutandis*, the efficiency frontier, the notions are not congruent. Because no account is taken of which goals are pursued, and because there is no presumption that particular goals ought to be promoted, the theory of justice as mutual advantage is not consequentialist. It follows, *pari passu*, that social welfare theory cannot accommodate this understanding of justice.

Even if it were supposed that social welfare theory and the justice as mutual advantage project could be reconciled, fundamental problems remain. First, serious questions attach to the 'original position' from which mutually advantageous bargaining is to proceed. As we shall see (§ 6.2), the notion that bargaining agents possess common and full knowledge of everyone's capabilities, endowments and preferences cannot be reconciled with fundamental features of observable reality. Second, it must be presumed that bargaining among narrowly self-interested agents will be characterized by opportunistic behavior. This, in turn, implies *ex ante* and *ex post* transaction costs; costs of which the theory takes no explicit account.[12] Third, even if these difficulties are set aside, the problem of respecting the adopted principles of justice (or 'conventions') is daunting:

> The reconciliation between morality and self-interest that mutual advantage theorists seek is hard to achieve, since the presence of rules of justice creates a classic prisoner's dilemma: even if you and I jointly benefit from the rules, I will do still better if you obey them and I allow myself to violate them when it suits me (Hausman and McPherson 1996, p. 159).

The difficulty is that, given that goals and the means of achieving them are neither right nor wrong, and given that agents are narrowly self-interested, nothing in the theory implies a duty to obey the rules of justice. While Gauthier (1986) argues that, given this prisoner's dilemma, it may be in agent A's interest to cultivate the kind of character in B that will lead B to obey the rules of justice, this leads to still other problems. In effect, the implicit suggestion that preferences and values are endogenously determined further erodes the plausibility of the original position.

Finally, if nothing in the theory implies respect for the adopted rules of justice, the same is true of rights. Because the theory does not regard individuals as having any inherent moral rights or status, it cannot accommodate the moral force of rights. While the problem here is similar to the conundrum confronting social welfare theorists, the 'rights' problem arises for mutual advantage theorists because 'rights flow from the constraints necessary for mutually beneficial cooperation, even when the activity in which people co-operate is the exploitation of other individuals' (Kymlicka 1993, p. 190).

The core problem, then, is that nothing in the mutual advantage formulation contemplates moral claims which are prior to the pursuit of mutual advantage. If one accepts the view that there are such prior moral claims – in particular, the moral equivalence of persons – then the theory of justice as mutual advantage is unacceptable. This is the perspective of the proponents of the Kantian/Rawlsian theory of justice as impartiality.[13]

## 2.22 Justice as Impartiality

As we have seen (§ 1.4), the theory of justice as impartiality is grounded in Kant's categorical imperative. Because proponents of the view of justice as impartiality take the moral equivalence of persons as given, justice demands the promotion of just institutions; principles or rules of the game which respect men as ends in themselves. As has been emphasized, the social contracts which give rise to the institutions do not justify the view of persons as ends in themselves. This is simply assumed. Granting this, in contrast to the mutual advantage construct, the contract device – the veil of ignorance (§ 1.5) – is used to negate rather than to reflect unequal bargaining power. Behind the veil of ignorance,

> The parties regard moral personality and not the capacity for pleasure and pain as the fundamental aspect of the self. They do not know what final aims persons have, and all dominant-end conceptions are rejected... The parties' aim in the original position is to establish just and favorable conditions for each to establish his unity. Their fundamental interest in liberty and in the means to make fair use of it is the expression of their seeing themselves primarily as moral persons with an equal right to choose their mode of life (Rawls 1971, p. 563).

In this account, rights are given lexical priority (§ 1.7), 'good outcomes' are neither defined nor promoted and, in contrast to consequentialist social welfare theory, the theory starts with a conception of the right, the moral law (§ 1.3). It is clear, therefore, that justice as impartiality cannot be accommodated by social welfare theory.

## 2.23 Sen's Consequentialist-Procedural Approach

Granting the logic of what has been said, consequentialist social welfare theory cannot accommodate the moral force of rights. It follows, *pari passu*, that it cannot accommodate a theory of justice as respect for rights. Moreover, as we have seen, neither contractarian understanding of justice is reconcilable with consequentialist social welfare theory.

A corollary of this is that social welfare theory can deploy only one standard of moral appraisal, efficiency. While the implications of this ethical poverty will be explored in later chapters, it is important that account be taken of an attempt to enrich social welfare theory's 'informational base'.

As we have seen, Amartya Sen rejects the notion of preference-independent, consequence-detached rights. While his effort to embed rights protections in consequences or 'state of affairs' is unavailing (§ 2.1), this is only one part of his consequentialist-procedural project. Equally important, his approach contemplates a particular understanding of justice.

Sen's point of departure is the 'informational poverty' of consequentialist social welfare theory (Klamer 1989, p. 140). While he is motivated in part by the force of Arrow's Possibility Result (§ 2.2), and in part by the interpersonal utility comparison problem (§ 6.5), Sen's central concern is that

> the 'informational base' of welfarism is too thin to support an acceptable – and perhaps even a coherent – account of the social good. If we are to generate a theory of the social good, we must accept the relevance of information about features of the world other than individuals' revealed preference (Sugden 1993, p. 1947).

Sen expands the informational base by adopting two conventions. On his view, 'living may be seen as consisting of a set of interrelated "functionings", consisting of beings and doings' (Sen 1992, p. 38). Thus, 'being adequately nourished' and 'being happy' are functionings. Understood in this way, functionings are an aspect of living, with comestibles merely instrumental to their achievement. A state of being, then, is understood to consist in a vector of functionings, and an agent's choice among such vectors determines the kind of life he lives. Finally, the set of feasible functioning vectors is the agent's capability set; the constraint which determines the agent's opportunity to achieve well-being.

While much can be said about this (Roth 1999, pp. 59–63), it is Sen's conception of justice which is of immediate interest. In his view, capabilities provide the most appropriate informational base for a theory of justice. Reduced to its essentials, Sen's theory of justice demands equality of capabilities. The essential point is that, given the logic of his approach, equal command over 'resources' – in the sense of income and wealth – does not imply equal opportunities in the sense of functionings. *Inter alia*, agents differ in their ability to convert resources into functionings. Granting this, it is better to base a theory of justice on capabilities, especially since resources have only a contingent value; a value based upon the opportunities to which they give rise.

If one grants both that resources like income and wealth do not have intrinsic value, and that it is opportunities that count for justice, then certain corollaries follow. First, because of their contingent value, interpersonal comparisons of income and wealth have no meaning, and phrases like 'equality of resources' are vacuous. Second, if Sen's equality of capabilities approach is to be operational, a metric must exist by which to measure the intrinsic value of functionings and capabilities. Given that well-being is a 'broad and partly opaque concept' which is intrinsically ambiguous (Sen 1992, pp. 46–49 and 134), it is not clear how such values would be determined. Moreover, if functionings have intrinsic value, information about individual's preferences and choices is unavailing. In view of these difficulties, it is 'natural to ask how far Sen's framework is operational' (Sugden 1993, p. 1953).

In sum, while Sen's consequentialist-procedural approach highlights the need for an expansion of the informational base of normative economics, he cannot logically derive the rights which he seeks to protect from desired consequences. Moreover, whatever else is said, it seems clear that the notional concepts embedded in his theory of justice do not have operational counterparts. Granting all of this, it is not clear that Sen has succeeded in expanding the 'moral reach' of social welfare theory. While his intent is to 'integrate procedural considerations in consequential analysis' (Sen 1995, p. 13) – a project which contemplates both rights and justice – efficiency remains the only dimension of moral appraisal to which social welfare theory gives rise.

## 2.24 Social Welfare Theory as a Time-Slice Principle of Justice

Given that right-based, contractarian and consequentialist-procedural understandings of justice cannot be accommodated by social welfare theory, the question becomes: Can *any* principle of justice be accommodated?

Recall first that the competitive equilibrium to which a perfectly competitive system is automatically impelled is, at a cross-section of time, one of an infinite number of Pareto-optimal or 'efficient' allocations. Which solution emerges – that is, which allocation is the competitive equilibrium – is determinate, given initial endowments, unattenuated property and exchange rights, and the instantaneously prevailing vector of product and input prices. Significantly, the initial endowment is not explained; it simply appears 'like manna from heaven'.

Assume, for simplicity, that the instantaneously prevailing competitive equilibrium happens also to be an ethical equilibrium (§ 2.2). Given that social welfare theory invokes no explicit principle of justice, what, if anything, can we say about this competitive-ethical equilibrium? Stated differently, does the theory invoke an *implicit* principle of justice?

In Robert Nozick's account, the answer is 'Yes':

> Welfare economics is the theory of current time-slice principles of justice. The subject is conceived as operating on matrices representing only current information about distribution. This, as well as some of the usual conditions (for example, the choice of distribution is invariant under a relabeling of columns), guarantees that welfare economics will be a current time-slice theory, with all of its inadequacies (1974, p. 154).

While Nozick's assessment invokes the language of game theory,[14] the essence of the argument is that: (a) 'all that needs to be looked at, in judging the justice of a distribution, is who ends up with what', with no account taken of how the distribution came about, and (b) 'any two structurally identical distributions are equally just'. We consider these two points seriatim:

First, no account is taken of how the competitive (and, presumably, ethical) equilibrium came about because nothing in the theory accounts for, or appraises the morality of, the initial endowment and the property and exchange right structure which, along with given relative prices, determine the unique, Pareto-optimal or efficient outcome. Second, the notion that two structurally identical distributions are equally just may be captured by appeal to Nozick's example: 'Two distributions are structurally identical if they present the same profile, but perhaps have different persons occupying the particular slots. My having ten and your having five, and my having five and your having ten are structurally identical distributions' (1974, p. 154).

Given that social welfare theory is utilitarian and that, *pari passu*, the desideratum is the maximization of aggregate welfare, the indifference among structurally identical distributions should come as no surprise. What is missing, of course, is a justification for such a view. Neither is a justification proffered for the (implicit) notion that how a distribution came about does not matter.

Granting all of this, I share Nozick's view that 'Most persons do not accept current time-slice principles as constituting the whole story about distributive shares' (1974, p. 154). The core problem is that end-result or end-state principles of distributive justice are unhistoric. At minimum, the forward and backward myopia of consequentialist social welfare theory implies a principle of justice for which no justification is proffered, and which, in any case, does not tell the whole story about distributive shares.

To sum up, consequentialist social welfare theory cannot accommodate the moral force of rights. It follows, *pari passu*, that it cannot regard justice as respect for rights. Moreover, it cannot accommodate a view of justice as mutual advantage or as impartiality. Finally, the time-slice or end-state principle of justice to which it implicitly gives rise is unacceptable. Granting all of this, the only standard for moral appraisal to which the theory gives rise is Pareto-optimality or efficiency. Unfortunately, as we shall see (Chapter 6), the efficiency standard is itself indeterminate.

## 2.3 CONSEQUENTIALISM AND THE CATEGORICAL IMPERATIVE

As we have seen, the categorical imperative or moral law is contractarian or procedural. Whereas consequentialist social welfare theory is consequence-based and procedurally detached, the categorical imperative demands that all persons be treated as morally equivalent. While social welfare theory cannot accommodate the moral force of rights, the categorical imperative demands that rights be respected. While social welfare theory is institutionless, the categorical imperative demands that just – in the sense of impartial – institutions be promoted. Finally, and fundamentally, because social welfare theory eschews a prior ethical commitment to the moral equivalence of persons – and all that it implies – it must rely on only one standard of ethical appraisal. Yet the imperative to promote Pareto-optimal or efficient outcomes cannot accommodate the lexical priority of rights, the principle of equal participation, or the imperative to provide rules of constitutional and conflictual politics which are consonant with the emergence of just – in the sense of impartial – legislation (§ 1.7). All of this has basic relevance to the discussion in Chapters 7, 8, 9 and 10.

## 2.4 CONTRACTARIANISM AND THE CATEGORICAL IMPERATIVE

Broadly speaking, both Hobbesian and Kantian contractarianism employ the social contract device, and both accept the view that persons are, by nature, equals (§ 1.4). While the former stresses equality of power and adduces a theory of justice as mutual advantage, the latter is grounded in the categorical imperative and regards justice as impartiality.

Given the logical and empirical difficulties attaching to the theory of justice as mutual advantage (§ 2.21), I shall adopt the Kantian/Rawlsian perspective and regard justice as impartiality. This perspective, along with an appreciation of the moral poverty and indeterminacy of the social welfare theoretic approach (Chapter 6), informs the balance of the book. Whereas social welfare theory deploys the outcomes-based efficiency standard to evaluate public policy (Chapters 3, 4 and 5), Kantian/Rawlsian contractarianism regards 'ends' or 'final aims' as subjective, assigns lexical priority to rights, and concentrates on the promotion of just institutions. Not surprisingly, the implications of this analysis for constitutional and conflictual politics differ sharply from those adduced from strict adherence to the efficiency standard.

# NOTES

1. See also Waldron (1995, p. 576).
2. Right- and goal-based moral theories may be distinguished as follows: 'The distinction between right-based and goal-based [moral] theories…is that a requirement is right-based if it is generated by a concern for some individual interest, goal-based if it is generated by a concern for something taken to be an interest of society as a whole' (Waldron 1995, p. 13). See also Dworkin (1978, p. 172).
3. Since, for libertarians, the point of rights is to protect liberty, 'considerations of welfare never justify interferences with individual liberty' (Hausman and McPherson 1993, p. 704). See also Waldron (1995, p. 19) and Nozick (1974).
4. For a discussion of the relationships among rights and utility, see Dworkin (1978, pp. 94–96).
5. For more on the logical difficulties with rule-utilitarianism, see Scruton (1994, pp. 282–283).
6. See Nozick (1974), especially pp. 150–160 for a discussion of his entitlement theory of justice.
7. When attention shifts to a comparative static analysis, it is easy to show that, given exogenously generated technical change, social welfare theory endorses a windfall ethic (Furubotn 1971). Finally, it is possible to argue that the theory does deploy an *implicit* 'time-slice' theory of justice. As Nozick (1974) emphasizes, however, the theory does not tell 'the whole story about distributive shares' (§ 2.24).
8. The 'simplifying assumptions' contemplate, *inter alia*, classical rationality, zero transaction costs, pure-rental type firms, and an institutionless decision environment (Furubotn and Richter 1991, pp. 11–12). A critical evaluation of this frictionless decision environment is the subject of Chapter 6.
9. In the situation envisioned, a well-behaved social welfare function generates a family of social indifference curves. By a familiar line of reasoning, a tangency of a social indifference curve and the efficiency frontier yields the unique, social welfare maximizing solution. For more on this, see Chapters 4 and 6.
10. As we have seen, because it cannot accommodate the moral force of rights, social welfare theory cannot accommodate the libertarian view of justice. It cannot, in other words, regard justice as respect for rights.
11. It is recognized that, to the extent that agent/bargainers possess heterogeneous capabilities, bargaining will result in asymmetric gains. It is assumed, moreover, that the bargaining process will itself yield gains. Whereas justice as mutual advantage would preserve the unequal gains that accrue as a result of prior advantages, the gains from cooperation would be distributed in accordance with a principle of 'minimax relative concession'. In effect, 'the largest concession anyone would have to make should be as small as possible' (Hausman and McPherson 1996, p. 159).
12. In a world characterized by bounded rationality, information asymmetries, opportunism and, *pari passu*, positive transaction costs, agents enter into relational or incomplete contracts (Furubotn and Richter 1997, pp. 158–160 and 478). *Inter alia*, these contracts seek to minimize the cost of *ex post* opportunism. Such contracts are clearly distinguishable from the classical contracts implicit in social welfare theory: 'In the neoclassical model, the characteristic transaction takes place instantaneously and the parties to it do not have any special interest in continued trade. Consequently, the understanding is that transactions are accomplished with the aid of the "complete" or "classical" contract' (Furubotn and Richter 1997, p. 477). The essential point is that the exchange contracts which generate the contract curves so central to social welfare theory are, in fact, classical contracts (p. 172).
13. For an additional critical appraisal of the theory of justice as mutual advantage, see Buchanan (1991, Chapter 16). See also Barry (1989, pp. 282–292). In Barry's account, a fundamental problem with justice as mutual advantage is its failure to provide any notion of justification. What is required is a view 'which makes agreement on reasonable terms

something of value in itself, rather than a more or less efficient means to the successful pursuit of one's ends' (p. 284). In his view, the premises which make such a view possible may be traced back to 'arguments advanced by David Hume and Adam Smith for an impartial standard of appraisal...' (p. 288). Barry suggests, then, 'that moral principles capable of passing the [justification] test proposed must have a certain quality of impartiality' (p. 290).

14. For a game-theoretic interpretation of Rawlsian justice, see Howe and Roemer (1981).

# 3. The consequentialist approach to government

## 3.1 UTILITARIANISM AS A STANDARD FOR JUDGING PUBLIC ACTION

We begin by recalling that, whereas contractarians do not start with a concept of the good, given independently of the right, consequentialists start with a view of what is good or valuable and specify that the proper response to those values is to promote them. We recall also that utilitarianism is the theory of the good which is most standardly deployed to fill out the consequentialist framework. Finally, we recognize that utilitarianism – whether in hedonistic, preference or welfare form[1] is 'first and foremost, a standard for judging public action'. By this account, 'the right action is that which maximizes utility (however construed) summed impersonally across all those affected by that action.... That is...the standard that public policy-makers are to use when making collective choices impinging on the community as a whole' (Goodin 1993, p. 245).

While the hedonistic pleasure–pain calculus advocated by Jeremy Bentham is today rarely, if ever, deployed, the essential point is that Bentham believed that only utilitarian arguments could justify political decisions (Dworkin 1978, p. 233). The same can be said of preference and welfare utilitarians. Whereas the former assert a public policy imperative to promote preference satisfaction, the latter 'would suppress short-sighted preference satisfaction in favor of protecting people's long-term welfare interests' (Goodin 1993, p. 244). In effect, welfare utilitarians embrace the idea that it is possible, *inter alia*, to determine what people 'need', rather than what they 'want' (Hausman and McPherson 1993, p. 706). Accordingly, public policy should promote 'welfare' or 'need' satisfaction.

## 3.2 UTILITARIANISM, POLITICS AND THE 'PUBLIC GOOD'

It is useful, again, to distinguish between constitutional and conflictual or day-to-day politics (§ 1.7). Because it is outcomes-based and procedurally detached, utilitarianism is ill-adapted to address the institutional issues contemplated by constitutional politics. While, in principle, rule-utilitarianism endorses rules which are justified on utilitarian grounds, utilitarian arguments can always be deployed to deviate from the rules (§ 2.1). Moreover, as we have seen, utilitarian theory cannot accommodate the moral force of rights. In effect, the constitutional rules of conflictual politics cannot, in the utilitarian framework, have force and effect. Finally, whereas the Kantian/Rawlsian contractarian enterprise contemplates a constitutional democracy (§ 1.7), the utilitarian justification of democratic institutions may best be characterized as tentative:

> the intellectual foundations of democratic institutions in [the utilitarian] perspective are weaker by an order of magnitude than those in the contractarian perspective. Democratic institutions stand or fall on their alleged superiority in generating the attainment of an independently existing 'public good' (Brennan and Buchanan 1985, p. 49).

It is characteristic of utilitarianism that there is no duty to respect rights or to promote just – in the sense of impartial – institutions. There is only a duty to promote 'good consequences'. From this perspective, both constitutional and conflictual politics are consequentialist and teleological. In effect, the only dimension of moral appraisal of political acts is a comparative assessment of their consequences (Davis 1993, p. 205). It follows, *pari passu*, that rather than seeking to 'get the institutions right', the utilitarian imperative is to promote the public good. As we have seen, a corollary of this is that utilitarians must regard democratic institutions as instrumentally rather than intrinsically valuable. If it could be shown that the public good can be more effectively promoted by, say, a monarchy, than by a constitutional democracy, then the former would be preferred to the latter. On this logic, moreover, constitutional constraints on the conflictual politics process may be perceived to inhibit promotion of the public good (Brennan and Buchanan 1985, p. 150).

If the institutional fluidity of the utilitarian approach is problematic, so too is the utilitarian conception of the public good. The key idea is that the good to be promoted – the public good – is understood to exist independently of the expression of individual values. This idea finds expression in the notion of a social preference or welfare function.

Kenneth Arrow (1951, p. 23) defined a social welfare function as a functional relationship that specifies a social ordering over all the social states for every set of individual preference orderings. While more will be said about this below (§§ 4.4 and 6.5), immediate interest centers on a fundamental, ontological problem. It is possible, in short, to question not only the transitivity of social preference, but the idea of social preference itself: 'rationality or irrationality as an attribute of the social group implies the imputation to that group of an organic existence apart from that of its individual components' (Buchanan 1954, p. 116).

While Professor Sen (1995, p. 5) concedes that, in light of Arrow's Possibility Result (§§ 2.2 and 6.5), Buchanan's objection is 'quite persuasive' when the idea of social preference connotes the operation of social decision mechanisms such as voting procedures, there is a sense in which this misses the point. The fundamental, ontological problem is not the transitivity of social preferences or of social decision mechanisms. The problem is that the utilitarian conception of the public good 'embodies a definition of "good" in application to the whole community of persons rather than to individual members'. It is, in short, a supraindividual 'good' to which is attributed an independent existence and which, moreover, must be promoted (Brennan and Buchanan 1985, p. 46). Given this understanding, the issue is not whether the utilitarian social welfare function is single-valued and consistently ordered. At issue is the presumption that the public good can have an 'external existence, outside the values and the evaluation activity of the person who is expressing himself through his [political] choice behaviour' (Brennan and Buchanan 1985, p. 42).

As we have seen, Amartya Sen regards Buchanan's ontological objection as 'quite persuasive'. In reaching this judgment he takes account of Arrow's Possibility Result, and has in mind a particular social preference construal. In his account, the ontological objection has force and effect when social preference connotes such social decision mechanisms as voting procedures. That said, Sen adopts the view that, the Possibility Result notwithstanding, when an individual expresses a social judgment he needs a concept like social preference. In effect, the social preference concept is instrumentally important to the expression of social judgments. On this view, the expression of social preferences is facilitated by the fact that, whereas interpersonal utility comparisons are 'not an easy thing to do in social-decision mechanisms', they 'can be used by a person making social welfare judgment, or in agreed procedures for social judgments…' (Sen 1995, p. 9).

That Professor Sen should espouse this view is not surprising. First, his implicit apologia for interpersonal utility comparisons is a part of his broader project. He seeks, *inter alia*, to overcome Arrow's Possibility Result by enriching social welfare theory's informational base (§ 2.23). Second, the emphasis on social welfare judgments is reflective of his commitment to a consequentialist-procedural approach to social welfare theory; an approach which seeks to provide an acceptable account of the 'social good' (§ 2.23).

In the event, I do not see how Sen's project overcomes either the impossibility of the Paretian liberal (§ 2.1) or Buchanan's ontological objection. Indeed, Sen's focus on the *individual's* invocation of social welfare judgments is not reconcilable with the notion of a supraindividual 'public good'.

The idea that individuals construct *internally conceived* notions of the 'public good' is, however, consistent with the contractarian approach:

> The contractarian model...depends[s]...on the presumption that the 'public good' or 'private good', or whatever mixture of these might be relevant, is internally conceived and hence is subjective to the person who acts. A person may...try to take into account the interests of all others in the community. But such interests enter as arguments in the choice calculus internally to the participant; the interests of others are imputed to them as estimated by the participant (Brennan and Buchanan 1985, p. 42).

The essential idea is that, whereas the utilitarian approach to politics relies on an organic, supraindividualistic notion of the public good, the contractarian model of politics 'depends not at all on the postulated motivation of the individual actor'. Indeed, 'any degree of "other-regardedness" can be incorporated, without difficulty, into the contractarian paradigm' (Brennan and Buchanan 1985, p. 42). That this is so follows from the Kantian/Rawlsian focus on institutional appraisal. What matters is that rights be given lexical priority, and that institutions be just (in the sense of impartiality). Stated differently, because the contractarian enterprise is both nonconsequentialist and deontological, the criteria of moral appraisal are applied to the processes of constitutional and conflictual politics rather than to end states. According to this, the arguments of individuals' maximands are subjective and not subject to prior specification (§ 2.4).

While the contractarian approach to government is the subject of Chapter 7, immediate interest centers on the fact that the contractarian paradigm can accommodate other-regardedness and, *pari passu*, an individuated, subjective perception of the public good. It follows that Sen's implicit claim that an individual's social judgement implies a supraindividual notion of social preference and, *mutatis mutandis*, a (presumably information-rich) social welfare function is incorrect. The Kantian/Rawlsian contractarian enterprise is fully accommodative of a notion of public good. An organic, supraindividualistic social welfare function is neither necessary nor sufficient for the emergence of social judgments. From the contractarian perspective, what *is* required is that rights be accorded lexical priority, and that the institutions of constitutional and conflictual politics be just. Given this decision environment, the political participant may then ask: 'Is Candidate A or Candidate B best for the whole community membership, in my own assessment of that question?' (Brennan and Buchanan 1985, p. 44).

The upshot is that Buchanan's ontological objection to the notion of a public good defined independently of the expression of individual values is, as Professor Sen suggests, 'quite persuasive'. This is true, as Sen makes clear, when the notion of social preference connotes the operation of a social decision mechanism. But it is also true if, as Sen argues, the expression of a social judgment requires a concept like social preference. The essential idea is that the conscious appraisal of public good (or 'public bad') reflects the intervention of *individual* rather than supraindividual values. This rudimentary fact calls into question the *organic existence* of a social welfare function.

## 3.3 INSTITUTIONAL AND ONTOLOGICAL PROBLEMS

The point of departure of this chapter is that utilitarianism is, first and foremost, a standard for judging public action. Given the utilitarian imperative to promote good consequences, attention centers on two issues. First, does the utilitarian paradigm imply a duty to respect the institutions which are justified on utilitarian grounds? As we have seen, the answer is no. Indeed, the utilitarian justification of constitutional democracy is contingent upon its perceived, relative success in promoting the public good. Second, in the utilitarian framework, the public good is understood to exist independently of the expression of individual values. In economists' hands, this idea is captured by a single-valued, consistently ordered social welfare function.

Given Arrow's well known Possibility Result, much attention has centered on the transitivity of the social welfare function, and on the operation of social decision mechanisms. It seems safe to say that much of the discussion proceeds on the presumption that the public good can have an external existence independent of the expression of individual values. Yet there appears to be no way around the ontological objection to this construal. Simply stated, the public good concept does not find an operational counterpart in a supraindividual social welfare function. Rather, it finds expression in the other-regardedness manifested in individual preference and value structures. This, in turn, is a central focus of the contractarian paradigm.

Given that it can neither accommodate a duty to respect instrumentally important institutions nor deploy an operational conception of the public good, utilitarian social welfare theory is an inappropriate standard for public policy appraisal.

## NOTE

1. See Section 2.1 for a discussion of rule-utilitarianism. Broadly speaking, rule-utilitarianism can be expressed in preference or welfare form. Its defining characteristic is that it contemplates institutions or 'rules' which are justified on utilitarian grounds.

# 4. Enter the economists

## 4.1 CONSEQUENTIALIST SOCIAL WELFARE THEORY

The 'economic' approach to government finds expression in the normative application of utilitarian social welfare theory. This, in turn, is a reflection of the 'relentlessly utilitarian' nature of economic theory's core ontology (Hahn 1982, p. 187).

Utilitarianism in the hands of economists differs, however, from the philosophical tradition. In particular, whereas 'ideal' utilitarians generally seek *a priori* the 'good' which should be promoted, economists identify welfare or the 'public good' with utility (Warke 2000, p. 374). Moreover, whereas Bentham's hedonic utilitarianism contemplated constitutional reforms intended to ensure that 'utilitarian processes would prevail in the public arena' (Warke 2000, p. 379), social welfare theory is institutionless. Finally, whereas utilitarianism is, perforce, a part of the corpus of moral philosophy, social welfare theory is *intendedly* value-free. All this notwithstanding, it remains true that utilitarianism as contemplated by most philosophers, and social welfare theory as deployed by economists are, first and foremost, theories of pubic action (§ 3.1).

## 4.2 EFFICIENCY AND EQUITY

Central to the social welfare theoretic enterprise is the distinction between 'efficiency' in the sense of Pareto optimality, and 'equity'. While the former contemplates the efficiency or welfare frontier, the latter involves appeal to the social welfare function.

While a critical appraisal of both constructs is deferred until Chapter 6, we have already encountered the social welfare function (Chapter 3). For the moment, our interest centers on the efficiency frontier.

As is well known, the instantaneously prevailing efficiency frontier is determinate, given the set of behavioral and technological postulates which characterize the frictionless neoclassical decision environment:

- Individual consumers are autonomous, atomistic, narrowly self-interested and classically rational utility maximizers. Their preferences are exogenously determined, stable, and defined on objects of choice whose technical, qualitative and property rights characteristics are known with certainty.

- The individual producer employs a single-equation, flow–flow production function which, *inter alia*, is presumed to be the only efficient or output-maximizing technical alternative available.
- Instrumentally important property and exchange rights are assumed to be unattenuated. In effect, the duties correlative to these rights are implicitly assumed to be respected.
- Given these assumptions, and given that all transactions are instantaneous, transaction costs are zero.
- Finally, as has been emphasized, neoclassical theory is both institutionless and intendedly value-free.

Achievement of points on the efficiency frontier – or, what is the same thing, of first-best Paretian optima – is predicated upon satisfaction of three 'welfare conditions'. In a barter economy the requirement is that: (1) the marginal rates of substitution of each pair of goods be the same for all consumers who consume the goods; (2) the marginal rates of technical substitution of each pair of inputs be the same for all employers of the inputs, and (3) the common marginal rates of substitution for each pair of goods must equal their respective marginal rates of physical transformation (along the production possibility frontier).

The link to an economy with money prices is affected on the presumption that all product and input markets are perfectly competitive. On this account, a defining characteristic of long-run perfectly competitive equilibrium is that it is Pareto-optimal. In effect, the fixity of product and input prices ensures the satisfaction of each of the three marginal equivalences and, *pari passu*, the attainment of a point on the efficiency frontier. The unique 'competitive equilibrium' to which the perfectly competitive system is impelled is determined, given the initial – and unexplained – resource endowment, by the instantaneously prevailing vector of product and input prices.

It is on this logic that the first fundamental welfare theorem asserts that a perfectly competitive system will automatically move to a first-best, Pareto-optimal or 'efficient' equilibrium (§ 2.2). Granting the logic of the approach, 'efficiency' becomes an instrument of public policy appraisal. *Ceteris paribus*, violations of one or more of the three welfare conditions constitute 'market failure' and may, therefore, call for government redress.

For its part, the second fundamental welfare theorem indicates that, no matter to which 'competitive' equilibrium the system is impelled, a 'socially desired' allocation can be realized by appeal to lump-sum taxes and bounties (§ 2.2).

As we have seen, determination of the 'socially desired' or 'ethical equilibrium' is predicated on the existence of a single-valued, consistently ordered social welfare function. While it is by no means clear that the ontological, empirical and other problems attaching to the notional social welfare function can be overcome,[1] let us suppose for the moment that it does have an empirical counterpart. Granting this – and setting aside the difficulties associated with 'lump sum' taxes and bounties (Graaff 1957, p. 78) – the second fundamental welfare theorem is regarded as having normative implications: Insofar as the instantaneously prevailing competitive equilibrium differs from the ethical equilibrium, government policy 'ought' to contemplate redistributional measures.

## 4.3 PUBLIC POLICY: THE FIRST AND SECOND FUNDAMENTAL WELFARE THEOREMS

Economists' propensity, explicitly or implicitly to invoke the two fundamental welfare theorems as a guide to government policy is well documented. The following quote is heuristic:

> At the most basic level, there can be only two rationalizations for the state's participation in an economy. The first is as a social equalizer, redistributing the fruits of a nation's production under the presumption that a particular social need takes precedence over private desires. The second justification for government participation is the assertion that markets fail to produce an efficient outcome (Jordan 2001, p. 22).

Whereas the 'second justification' clearly invokes the efficiency standard and, *pari passu*, the first fundamental welfare theorem, the first is predicated on the notion of a 'social need'. Insofar as social need is understood to be synonymous with public good, the first rationalization implicitly assumes the ontological existence of a supraindividual 'good' which must be promoted. As we have seen, this idea is captured by the notional social welfare function (§ 3.2).

If Jordan's view is heuristic, Joseph Stiglitz's thinking is quite explicit:

> As a long-time student of the public sector, I welcomed the opportunity to come to Washington as a member of the Council of Economic Advisers and later to become the Chairman of the Council....
> To be sure, I came as an activist...with a view about what it was that government should, and should not be doing. My reference point was the fundamental theorems of welfare economics...it has been shown that in the presence of imperfect information or incomplete markets, the economy will not be Pareto efficient; in other words, there will always be some intervention by which the government can make everyone better off.... (1998, pp. 3–4).

While it must be acknowledged that a 'New Political Economy' literature has recently grown up which 'departs from the assumption often made in conventional economics that policy is determined by maximizing a social welfare function' (Saint-Paul 2000, p. 915), the view is still dominant among economists that 'The measurement of welfare forms the foundation of public policy analysis' (Slesnick 1998, p. 2108). Indeed, Geoffrey Brennan has argued that

> The point of departure for the economist's theory of the state is a set of propositions about 'market success'. In their modern welfare economics variant, these propositions revolve around the claim that perfectly competitive markets generate a Pareto optimal outcome.... It is common for economists to identify a direct intellectual line in such reasoning from Adam Smith, through David Ricardo, to the formal theorems of the Arrow-Debreu general equilibrium models.... (1995, p. 142).[2]

That the economist's theory of the state – effectively summarized by the two fundamental welfare theorems[3] – should be traced to Adam Smith is perhaps not surprising. Smith's 'invisible hand' metaphor ([1776] 1976, p. 456) is, after all, intended to show the positive, unintended consequences of the market; of the channelling of self-interest into collective benefits. Yet, it is also clear that Smith wrote *The Wealth of Nations* 'to encourage legislators to resist the pressures of economic groups attempting to use political power to advance their own interests' (Muller 1993, p. 204). Accordingly, Smith's emphasis was less on market imperfections which, presumably, 'require' government intervention, than on 'the role of government and law in strengthening the social institutions that foster self-control and benevolence' (Muller 1993, p. 126). In this account, the government 'performs its economic role by providing the legal framework within which the market can coordinate economic behavior for the public benefit'. But it also plays a role in encouraging moral behavior (Muller 1993, pp. 111–112).

The essential point is that, whereas Adam Smith emphasized the role and importance of formal and informal institutions – including ethical constraints – in the functioning of markets, the two fundamental welfare theorems are more narrowly construed. In particular, the two theorems have no institutional content. Whereas the Pareto criterion – the first fundamental welfare theorem – relies on unattenuated exchange and property rights, the theory simply assumes that the duty to respect these rights will be respected. That said, on the presumption that such rights might *not* be respected, social welfare theorists do acknowledge the state's constitutional role. On this account, the state must, *inter alia*, provide and enforce a rule of law. Yet, as we have seen, utilitarian arguments can always be deployed to deviate from the rules which themselves are justified on utilitarian grounds (§ 2.1). In effect, whatever rules are promulgated, no utilitarian argument can be deployed which demands respect for those rules. Indeed, as we shall see, a literature has grown up which suggests that corruption can be 'efficient' (Chapter 5). Finally, the first fundamental welfare theorem is frequently invoked to justify both 'regulatory' interventions – given the market's failure to satisfy one or more of the three marginal equivalences – and the provision of public goods; goods which are nonexclusive in consumption (Buchanan 1968). Broadly speaking, the focus of these imperatives is not to 'get the institutions right'. It is to 'get the prices right'.

For its part, the second fundamental welfare theorem relies on a comparison of competitive and ethical equilibria (§ 2.2). While the theory emphasizes the efficacy of lump-sum taxes and bounties in reconciling the equilibria, no explicit theory of justice is invoked. Given that 'justice' is a procedural notion (§ 2.2), it follows that the absence of an explicit understanding of justice implies an institutional void. Granting this, appeal to the second fundamental theorem does not suggest an institutional imperative. More fundamentally, social welfare theory cannot, in any case, accommodate theories of justice as respect for rights, as mutual advantage or as impartiality (Chapter 2).

In the face of this definitional and institutional void the public policy implications of the second fundamental welfare theorem are indeterminate. At most, social welfare theorists seem generally inclined to agree that: (1) a first-best Pareto optimal allocation is not necessarily a 'just' distribution, and (2) the redistribution activities of the state 'tend to upset the capacity of the market system to mobilize gains from exchange; hence [there is an] "efficiency-equity tradeoff"' (Brennan 1995, p. 143). Granting this, it is not clear what social welfare theory has to say about distributive justice. Even if one sets aside the logical, empirical and other problems associated with the efficiency frontier and the social welfare function (Chapter 6), the second fundamental welfare theorem cannot *meaningfully* be deployed as an instrument of moral appraisal. In sum, social welfare theorists are effectively left with the first fundamental welfare theorem and, *pari passu*, reliance on the efficiency standard.

## 4.4 WHAT SHOULD THE GOVERNMENT DO?

Granting the logic of what has been said, the only evaluative standard available to social welfare theorists is the Pareto criterion. It is, in fact, a standard which economists have not been reluctant to employ. Indeed, it is possible to argue that some economists have proceeded on the implicit assumption that, in the face of 'market failure', the government can, necessarily, do better: '...welfare economists may sometimes have fallen into the trap of arguing that, if the market fails, the government is sure to do better...thereby making welfare economics and its applications much more progovernment and prointerference than could be justified on scientific grounds' (Sandmo 1990, p. 58).[4]

As we shall see, the fundamental problem with the efficiency standard is that it is, in fact, indeterminate (Chapter 6). Yet, even if one were to grant that the standard has basic relevance, it remains true that '...to recommend public action to correct for market failure requires a positive theory of government behavior to convince us that there is in fact reason to expect that the government will do better than the market. Sometimes, no doubt, it will do worse' (Sandmo 1990, p. 59).

Plainly stated, the requisite 'positive' theory of government does not exist. On the contrary, a body of theory questions the 'benevolent despot' model of government implicit in social welfare theory. The essence of the public choice approach is a rejection of the assumption that, whereas man is self-interested in market activity, he 'suppresses these motives and brings out the more "noble" ones in his political behavior' (Buchanan [1962] 1999, pp. 68–69). In effect, public choice theorists regard the '"benevolent despot" model of government...as hopelessly at odds with assumptions made elsewhere in economics about human motivations and social institutions' (Brennan 1995, p. 147).

If social welfare theory implicitly assumes that 'government' may be modelled as a single, benevolent, decision-maker, it also ignores the intervention of political institutions (Salanié 2000, pp. 8–9). In reality, government policy decisions emerge as a result of an intertemporal political process in which account is taken of many, sometimes competing, interests. From this perspective it is not at all clear that what animates the political process is an explicit accounting of a supraindividual 'socially desired' outcome. According to this, the maximand is not a social welfare function. Rather, the political decision environment contemplates multiple objective functions and constraints – and frequently opaque decision processes. It is, in short, the decision environment contemplated by Adam Smith, an environment characterized, *inter alia*, by information asymmetry and by opportunistic behavior.

Once explicit account is taken of the objective features of the 'political process' the benevolent despot formulation is hopelessly inadequate, and palpably absurd. What is required is an empirically richer model in which principals cannot always effectively monitor their agents' behavior,[5] multiple subjectively-defined desiderata militate against the specification of a 'socially desired' outcome, and 'political economy' contemplates the institutions of both constitutional and conflictual politics. While outcomes-based, procedurally detached social welfare theory is ill-suited to this project, the Kantian/Rawlsian contractarian enterprise contemplates a set of institutional imperatives: Whereas utilitarian social welfare theory provides only a contingent defense of constitutional democracy, the Kantian/Rawlsian contractarian justification is unqualified (§§ 1.7 and 3.2). Whereas utilitarian social welfare theory cannot accommodate the moral force of rights, the Kantian/Rawlsian approach assigns lexical priority to rights (§§ 2.1 and 2.22). Whereas utilitarian social welfare theory does not entertain – and cannot accommodate – any plausible understanding of justice (Chapter 2), the Kantian/Rawlsian approach contemplates a duty to promote just, in the sense of impartial, institutions (§ 1.7). In effect, while the social welfare theorist imagines that a benevolent despot will pursue a supraindividual, 'socially desired' outcome, the Kantian/Rawlsian contractarian seeks institutional arrangements which reflect the moral equivalence of persons. On this account, the individual is free to pursue his political ends – whatever they may be – subject to the constraints imposed by rights protections and the impartial treatment of individuals (Chapter 7).

## NOTES

1. See, especially, Sections 2.1 and 2.23, and Chapters 3 and 6.
2. Mark Blaug suggests that the publication of the 1954 Arrow-Debreu paper 'proving the existence of general equilibrium', and Paul Samuelson's 1955 announcement of the 'neoclassical synthesis' [mark] the 'true birth of what has ever since been called "neoclassical economics"' (Blaug, 2001, p. 161).
3. Slesnick (1998, p. 2139) has argued that, in view of Arrow's Possibility Result, 'if one precludes interpersonal utility comparisons of welfare...welfare economics became completely summarized by the two Fundamental Theorems of Welfare Economics relating competitive equilibria to Pareto optimality'.
4. See also Brennan and Buchanan ([1985] 2000, pp. 129–130). Interestingly, even economists engaged in social welfare theoretic public policy appraisal are cognizant of the theory's 'rather rosy view of government' (Rosen 1999, pp. 112 and 123–124). For a similar view see Stiglitz (1988, pp. 82–83).
5. For a discussion of the 'agency' role of elected representatives, see Hampton (1995, pp. 391–392).

# 5. The efficiency standard, corruption and the growth of government

## 5.1 'EFFICIENCY-ENHANCING' CORRUPTION

The philosopher Roger Scruton has suggested that Jeremy Bentham's 'felicific calculus' is the 'archetype of the decision theory that is now accepted in economics' (1994, p. 283). Whether or not this is correct, it is his criticism of consequentialism in its utilitarian form that is of immediate interest.

In Scruton's account, utilitarian morality is the morality of homo economicus – the classically rational, narrowly self-interested agent of neoclassical economic theory (Chapters 4 and 6). While he does not reject the Smithian 'invisible hand' and, *pari passu*, the notion that 'Free transactions by profit seeking individuals [unintendedly] benefit society', he sees these benefits as contingent upon the intervention of 'interdictions': 'Cheating, fraud, theft and the like must be forbidden' (1994, p. 283). Broadly speaking, this thinking is consistent with the view that 'A market economy is perhaps best viewed as a network of rights and obligations based on contracts and legal requirements' (Furubotn and Richter 1997, p. 140).

To some, the claim that ethical constraints are instrumentally, even intrinsically, valuable to the functioning of market economies may seem unexceptionable. Indeed, the transaction cost economics literature is predicated, *inter alia*, on the idea that 'bounded rationality and opportunism are characteristic features of the real world' (Furubotn and Richter 1997, p. 166). It follows that ethical constraints may both reduce transaction costs and facilitate exchange in increasingly impersonal markets (Arrow 1969, p. 62).

All of this has basic relevance to Scruton's critique of the utilitarian account of morality. Because utilitarianism – and, *mutatis mutandis*, utilitarian social welfare theory – is consequentialist, 'morality is justified by its beneficial effects'. Therefore, from the utilitarian perspective

> we should adjust and amend [morality] in the light of these effects. If, in this or that circumstance, I can apprehend an overwhelming benefit that follows from flouting a principle, or an overwhelming disaster that flows from obeying it, I ought to disobey. Principles must always be weighed against consequences if morality is to be rational.... Moral 'absolutism' is even castigated as a crime. In this way, through the theory of 'consequentialism', the possibility of unlimited

> corruption has re-entered the modern conscience and produced some interesting casuistry in 'applied ethics' (Scruton 1994, p. 283).

We have already encountered the idea that utilitarian theory and, *pari passu*, social welfare theory, cannot accommodate the moral force of rights (§ 2.1). While Scruton's account of utilitarian morality is consistent with that discussion, it is his claim that the theory has 'produced some interesting casuistry in "applied ethics"' that is of particular interest.

It is clear that utilitarian social welfare theory is a part of the corpus of 'applied ethics' (§ 1.1). And, it seems, it has been subject to some 'interesting casuistry'.

As we saw in Section 2.1, social welfare theorists must either argue that the exchange and property rights which they regard as instrumentally important are morally exigent in themselves – and reject the efficiency standard – or deploy the efficiency standard and reject the moral force of rights. What seems clear is that some economists have adopted the latter approach. To see this, we need only appeal to the literature which suggests that corruption may be 'efficiency-enhancing'.

While it must be said that there is a literature which suggests that corruption may be negatively associated with private investment and growth (Mauro 1995), there is also the view that the 'informal sector' may contribute 'to the creation of markets, increase financial resources, enhance entrepreneurship, and transform the legal, social, and economic institutions necessary for accumulation' (Asea 1996, p. 166). If this is a somewhat oblique invocation of the 'efficiency-enhancing' effects of corruption, others have been more explicit. Lui has suggested, for example, that 'corruption is an optimal response to market distortions and may improve allocative efficiency' (1996, p. 26). While Lui invokes 'market distortions', others regard the second best world characterized by regulatory policy-induced 'distortions' as fertile ground for 'efficiency-improving corruption' (Bardhan 1997, p. 1322). Indeed, according to Braguinsky, 'The literature has pointed out that some forms of corruption are more detrimental to growth, while others can be considered even beneficial, given the underlying regulation' (1996, p. 14).

If some economists deploy the theory of second best (Lipsey and Lancaster 1956) to argue that corruption may be efficiency-enhancing, there are those who argue that the constrained utility maximization postulate *implies* corrupt behavior:

> all individuals, government officials and politicians without exception, are constrained self-maximizers....each and every politician and government official has only one priority in mind. Just like you and me, they get up in the morning and think about how to produce more income for themselves, and under the usual

> social and political constraints corruption is generally the most convenient avenue to achieve the goal (Cheung 1996, p. 1).

Consistent with this general theme, Gordon Tullock has suggested that 'Most people who object to corruption probably do so on moral grounds without considering the practical effects' (1996, p. 7). In his view, the 'moral objection' misses the point: 'corruption...may have some redeeming features. It may make possible smaller or no salary payments to [government] officials who, if carefully supervised, will still carry out their functions on a fee-for-service basis' (1996, p. 6).[1]

The propensity of some economists to regard corruption as potentially efficiency-enhancing may properly be regarded as an example of the 'interesting casuistry' to which utilitarian morality gives rise.[2] The essential point is that, because utilitarian social welfare theory is consequence-based and procedurally detached, the theory may be employed to 'justify' any means to achieve 'efficient' outcomes. Significantly, the utilitarian view that morality is circumstantial or contingent has informed the thinking of the Chicago School of Law and Economics. For example, Richard Posner's 'adaptionist [or functionalist] conception of morality, in which morality is judged...by its contribution to the survival, or other ultimate goals, of a society or some group within it' (1999, p. 6) is clearly utilitarian. Not surprisingly, members of the Chicago School focus on efficiency, and argue that there is a duty to promote it. Indeed, in Posner's account justice *is* efficiency (1975, p. 777).

While the external and internal morality of the law will be taken up in Chapter 8, it is sufficient for present purposes to recall that justice is a procedural notion (§ 2.2). It is, in short, a concept which cannot be subsumed by the marginal equivalences which define an efficient outcome. That said, there is a larger point to be made: On the one hand, some social welfare theorists argue that corruption is 'efficiency-enhancing'. On the other hand, a leading scholar of the 'Chicago School' of law and economics argues that efficiency is justice. Clearly, Scruton's view that consequentialism has 'produced some interesting casuistry in "applied ethics"' has basic relevance.

It is useful now to recall that social welfare theorists regard unattenuated property and exchange rights as instrumentally important to the achievement of first-best Paretian or 'efficient' outcomes. That the theory should be deployed to rationalize efficiency-enhancing corruption gives rise to a logical conundrum: Either rights must be respected, so that corruption is inadmissible, or corruption is endorsed, and efficiency cannot be achieved.

As has been repeatedly emphasized, the fact that utilitarian social welfare theory cannot regard rights as having moral force militates against any understanding of rights as side constraints on action (§ 2.1). Moreover, it is clear that the implicit endorsement of corruption is not reconcilable with any plausible understanding of justice, whether rights-protection, mutual advantage or impartiality (Chapter 2). The root cause of the problem is that utilitarian social welfare theory is consequence-based and procedurally detached. The fact that it incorporates elements of goal- and right-based moral theories is unavailing precisely because the theories cannot be reconciled. What is clearly missing in the theory is a justification of the duty to respect the rights which social welfare theory *cannot* justify on utilitarian grounds. That such a theory is questionable on moral grounds is self-evident. That it should be employed as a standard for public policy appraisal is, at best, problematic.

## 5.2 MARKET 'IMPERFECTIONS' OR 'GETTING THE PRICES RIGHT'

Almost four decades ago James Buchanan suggested that 'economists tend to be so enmeshed with efficiency notions that it seems extremely difficult for them to resist the ever-present temptation to propose yet more complex gimmicks and gadgets for producing greater "efficiency"' ([1962] 1999, p. 62). Given economists' continuing propensity to invoke 'market imperfections' to justify government market interventions, the remark might just as appropriately be made today.

Granting this, two preliminary observations should be offered. First, in their relentless efforts to 'apply' social welfare theory, economists may have forgotten that the theory is predicated, *inter alia*, upon the existence not only of a benevolent despot (Chapter 4), but of an 'omniscient being – the observing economist'. On this account, the omniscient observing economist 'possesses whatever information we may require about tastes, techniques, the future, and anything else' (Graaff 1957, p. 13). Graaff clearly intended the omniscient being as an 'expository device' – as a generative assumption which, for *predictive* purposes, need not be 'realistic' (Roth 1998, Chapter 1). It is at least arguable that, in the hands of welfare economists, a generative assumption has metamorphosed into a presumptive description of reality. Suffice it to say that, to the extent that invocations of the efficiency standard are animated by the assumption that the observing economist is 'omniscient', the recipient of the advice – the benevolent despot – will, himself, require a willing suspension of disbelief. Second, Buchanan's remark was published six years after the appearance of Lipsey and Lancaster's 'The General Theory of Second Best' (1956). As we saw in Chapter 4, the attainment of a first-best Paretian optimum requires satisfaction of the marginal equivalences or 'Paretian conditions'. With this as background,

> The general theorem for the second best optimum states that if there is introduced into a general equilibrium a constraint which prevents the attainment of one of the Paretian conditions, the other Paretian conditions, although still attainable, are in general no longer desirable. In other words, given that one of the Paretian optimum conditions cannot be fulfilled, then an optimum situation can be achieved only by departing from all the other Paretian conditions (Lipsey and Lancaster, 1956, p. 11).

The 'negative corollary' of the theorem is that 'it is *not* true that a situation in which more, but not all, of the optimum conditions are fulfilled is necessarily, or is even likely to be, superior to a situation in which fewer are fulfilled' (ibid., p. 12). Granting all of this, Lipsey and Lancaster suggest that

> It should be obvious...that the principles of the general theory of second best show the futility of 'piecemeal welfare economics'. To apply to only a small part of an economy welfare rules which would lead to a Paretian optimum if they were applied everywhere, may move the economy away from, not toward, a second best optimum position (p. 17).

The point at issue here is not whether the efficiency standard is determinate. In fact, it is not (Chapter 6). Rather, the point is that, if one accepts social welfare theory *on its own terms*, the general theorem of the second best 'show[s] the futility of "piecemeal welfare economics"'. Whatever else is said, whether diagnosed 'market-failure' problems fall under the rubric of generalized externalities, public goods, or 'monopoly elements', policy prescriptions are, inevitably, 'piecemeal': While 'regulatory' policy initiatives may be informed by general equilibrium theory, explicit account cannot be taken of all of the interrelationships which characterize an economy (Salanié 2000, p. 138).

Consider now the implications for the application of the efficiency standard. On the one hand, social welfare theory assumes that the economist-policy adviser is omniscient. It follows, *pari passu*, that the adviser must apprehend the objective features of observable reality; of a 'world where many imperfections exist and only a few can be removed at any one time' (Lipsey and Lancaster 1956, p. 13). Yet, on the other hand, this is precisely the decision environment to which the general theory of second best applies. It is a world, in other words, in which 'the principles of the general theory of second best show the futility of "piecemeal welfare economics"'.

Despite this evident, logical conundrum, and despite Buchanan's (1962) admonition that 'it seems extremely difficult for [economists] to resist the ever-present temptation to propose yet more complex gimmicks and gadgets for producing greater "efficiency"', the temptation persists. The contemporary view has been summarized by Viscusi, Vernon and Harrington:

> Ideally, the purpose of antitrust and regulation policies is to foster improvements judged in efficiency terms. We should move closer to the perfectly competitive ideal than we would have in the absence of this type of intervention. The objective is to increase the efficiency with which the economy operates, recognizing that we may fall short of the goal of replicating a perfectly competitive market, but nevertheless we can achieve substantial improvements over what would prevail in the absence of such government intervention (2000, p. 9).

While much can be said about this, immediate interest centers on the implicit presumption, already noted (§ 4.4), that 'if the market fails, the government is sure to better'. *Inter alia*, the problem is that the 'benevolent despot' formulation both denies the basic relevance of self-interested behavior and ignores the intervention of political institutions. Fundamentally, the model ignores the intervention of political processes which, presumptively, affect and are affected by the self interest of politicians, bureaucrats and voter-principals. Granting this,

> There is no necessary presumption that simply because markets are imperfect, political processes will work better. On the contrary, as public-choice theory reminds us, there are very good reasons for doubting the capacity of political processes to achieve Pareto optimatility. The normatively relevant comparison is between two imperfect institutions. The mere observation that one institution or the other is imperfect – that markets 'fail' – is simply not sufficient to establish a case for government 'intervention' (Brennan and Buchanan 1985, p. 130).

Let us, once again, set aside the fundamental objection to deployment of the efficiency standard; namely, that it is indeterminate. This is the subject matter of Chapter 6. Consider, then, the familiar problem of generalized externalities; of divergences between marginal private cost (MPC) and marginal social cost (MSC).

As is well known, appeal to the efficiency standard suggests that, in the presence of an external diseconomy (MSC > MPC), a Pareto optimal tax may result in an efficient outcome.[3] Alternatively, the presence of an external economy (MSC < MPC) suggests the payment of a Pareto optimal subsidy.

Assume the case of an external diseconomy. In the event, the problem for 'government' is to determine the amount of the corrective tax. This, in turn, requires appeal to objective measurements of both MSC and MPC. Suppose, for example, that some effluent has reduced air quality. As Buchanan has shown ([1969] 1999, p. 67), because 'clean air' cannot be traded or exchanged, 'There is no possibility of marginal adjustments over quantities of the "good" so as to produce an equilibrium that ensures against interpersonal differences in relative evaluations'. Granting this, MSC is not objectively measurable.

Measurement difficulties also attach to MPC. Whereas the efficiency analysis implicitly assumes that money outlays inform the choices made by the source of the external diseconomy, observed money outlays need not reflect choice influencing costs. Absent a perfectly competitive long-run equilibrium, there can be no presumption that quasi-rents are absent. It follows that, under conditions of imperfect competition – the conditions which obtain in the 'real world' – 'there can be no presumption that anticipated outlay measures subjective opportunity costs, those that must influence actual choice behavior' (Buchanan [1969] 1999, p. 70). Moreover, it is possible that the 'polluter' may be other-regarding in the sense that his subjective assessment of private costs includes an imputation for the costs imposed on other, affected parties (Buchanan [1969] 1999, pp. 71–74). In this circumstance, outlays do not measure the polluter's subjective opportunity costs. In effect, the assumption implicit in Pigovian efficiency analysis – that observed outlays reflect choice-influencing costs – requires that quasi-rents be absent, and that polluters be narrowly self-interested. Granting the logic of the approach, relaxation of one or both of these restrictions implies that observed outlays underestimate the subjectively determined costs which influence choice. Given these complexities there can be no presumption that 'the government' can determine *the* 'Pareto optimal' tax. It follows, *pari passu*, that there can be no presumption that 'the government can do better' than the market.

Even if these complexities were set aside, it remains true that the presumed efficacy of government intervention is predicated on the assumption that, while 'bifurcated man' is narrowly self-interested in his market activity, he evinces 'noble' motives in his political behavior. According to this, the individual's political activity reflects his view of the 'public' or 'social' interest. Suppose, however, that in the presence of externalities a less-than-unanimity rule collective choice process unfolds in which, in his *political* (as well as his market behavior), the individual is narrowly self-interested. Under the circumstances envisioned,

> In the calculus of the individuals making the final collective decision, marginal private benefits will tend to exceed marginal social benefits and/or marginal private costs will tend to fall short of marginal social costs. The distortions produced are, therefore, precisely analogous, in opposing directions, to those present in the market solution characterized by the familiar Pigovian divergences…the value of a political vote…lies in its potential power to impose external costs on other members of the group (Buchanan [1962] 1999, p. 65).

Suppose now that, under the same market and voting rule conditions, the voter is other-regarding in the sense that he 'tries to act in the genuine interest of the whole group as this is determined for him through the application of some appropriately-chosen Kantian-like rule of action' (Buchanan [1962] 1999, p. 67). In effect, we assume that, as in Chapter 1, the individual regards each person as morally equivalent. Under the circumstances envisioned, then, each person's rights are respected, and each person is treated impartially. It follows that 'no deliberate exploitation of minority can take place', and 'The Pigovian divergence between marginal private product and marginal social product disappears in both the market and the political organization of activity….' ([1962] 1999, pp. 67–68).

Granting the logic of what has been said, the efficacy of government intervention in the face of market failure depends on a peculiar asymmetry. Man is presumed to be self-interested in market behavior, but both omniscient and beneficent in his political activity!

Consider now the case of public goods; of goods which, in the limit, are nonexclusive in consumption. As is well known, it is a defining characteristic of a genuinely collective or public good or service that it is indivisible in consumption. It follows that persons cannot adjust their individual purchases over varying quantities. Yet, because different persons will place different marginal values on a given quantity of the good or service, 'If each person is to be in equilibrium in the sense that, for him, the quantity supplied is that which he prefers, differentials in marginal prices must be introduced' (Buchanan [1968] 1999, p. 32).

Assume now that the 'bifurcated man' assumption is dropped. Assume, in other words, that man is narrowly self-interested in both his market and in his political activity. It follows that, if the public good is privately provided, significant externalities will be present: In his private behavior, the individual will take account of his share of the total marginal benefit, and equate that with the total marginal cost of the good's provision. The public good will therefore be 'underproduced', and the Pigovian efficiency standard may be deployed to argue for public provision of the public good or service. On the presumption, however, that the good is provided by the public sector, satisfaction of the efficiency standard requires that a vector of optimal tax-prices be institutionalized. In effect, politically organized provision of a genuinely public good or service requires price-discrimination across effective demanders of the good: 'each individual shall be required to contribute a "tax-price" that is exactly proportional to his own marginal rate of substitution between the collective good and money (all other goods)' (Buchanan [1962] 1999, p. 71).

Whatever else might be said about this, two observations seem appropriate. First, even if it were supposed that the self-interested public provider were *willing* to price-discriminate, 'the fine discrimination dictated by such conditions can hardly be achieved' (Buchanan [1968] 1999, p. 123).[4] Second, given the incentive for the self-interested government agent to *avoid* price discrimination, a constitutional restraint may be required. *Inter alia*, the constitution might require that genuinely public goods or services be provided by the public sector, and that such goods and services 'shall be financed by taxes that are levied on the "marginal benefit principle"' (Buchanan [1962] 1999, pp. 70–71. Yet, because of informational requirements, a constitutional restraint may be unavailing. *Inter alia*, the 'fine discrimination' contemplated 'would require that the taxing authorities be able to determine, in advance, all individual preference functions' (Buchanan [1962] 1999, p. 73). Even in the case in which a genuinely public good or service may be treated as an input in firms' production functions, the specification of [derived] demand functions is a daunting matter (Roth 1979).

What, then, may be said about governmental provision of public goods or services? Buchanan has summarized the situation in this way:

> Even for those goods and services that are wholly collective in nature, the provision of them through the political process will produce Pigovian-like externalities at the margin unless taxes are collected on the basis of marginal benefits. In the real world, very few, if any, goods and services are wholly collective. And even if these few could be isolated, they would not be financed by taxes levied on this principle of incremental benefits enjoyed. Such a principle is not only politically unimaginable in modern democracy; it is conceptually impossible (Buchanan [1962] 1999, p. 73).

On this logic it seems clear that public provision of a genuinely public good 'must embody externalities', even in the case of a constitutionally imposed requirement that taxes be levied according to the marginal benefit principle.[5]

In summary, market provision of public goods and services does, in fact, violate the efficiency standard. That said, there can be no presumption that 'government' can do better. Reduced to its essentials, the idea which emerges from this is that appeal to the efficiency standard admits of the possibility of market *and* political imperfections.

If appeals to the presence of generalized externalities and public goods and services are frequently the catalysts to calls for government intervention, so too are 'monopoly elements'. Recognizing that, at the Pareto-optimal or efficient long-run perfectly competitive equilibrium price (P) equals marginal cost (MC), it has become commonplace to employ the static or single-period Lerner index to 'measure monopoly power'. The index, the mark-up ratio of price minus marginal cost to price, or (P – MC/P), may take any value from zero to one. For the perfectly competitive firm P = MC so that the index takes the value zero. On this account, the larger the value of the index 'the greater the degree of monopoly power' and, *pari passu*, the more 'inefficient' the price-output solution (Pindyck and Rubinfeld 1997, pp. 347–348).

Difficulties with the Lerner index of 'monopoly power' abound. *Inter alia*, as Pindyck and Rubinfeld suggest, 'the index ignores dynamic aspects of pricing such as effects of the learning curve, shifts in demand, etc.' (1997,

p. 348, fn 6). It is, in fact, relatively easy to show that, when the desideratum is intertemporal profit maximization, learning-by-doing and demonstration effects require a departure from the single-period decision rule, that marginal revenue equal marginal cost (Roth 1995). In the event, violation of the efficiency standard is not *prima facie* evidence of monopoly power. It is merely a response to prevailing market conditions.

The key idea is that the Lerner index is a measure of static inefficiency. Once allowance is made for intertemporal phenomena the index is not unambiguously interpretable. For example, while endogenously generated technological change is logically irreconcilable with perfect competition, it is observable in 'real world', imperfectly competitive markets. Yet, as Mansfield and Yohe have suggested, 'the static inefficiency of an imperfectly competitive economy could be offset over time if it had a higher rate of technological change and productivity growth' (2000, pp. 575–576).

If dynamic considerations militate against the use of the efficiency standard, there is an even more fundamental difficulty. As was emphasized in Chapter 4, the decision environment which generates the Paretian welfare equivalences is 'frictionless'. *Inter alia*, classically rational and fully informed 'entrepreneurs' are assumed to employ the only efficient – or output maximizing – technical alternative available. In fact, the decision environment which is characteristic of observable reality contemplates bounded rationality (Conlisk 1996) and positive transaction costs. While more will be said about this in Chapter 6, immediate interest centers on the resultant technical environment. The threshold idea is that a boundedly rational producer – that is, a producer who is not omniscient and has difficulty processing information – does not, at a cross-section of time, possess exhaustive knowledge of the available technical options (Roth 1972, 1977). Given that a product may be produced via the employment of one or more of a set of alternative production functions, the presumption is that the boundedly rational producer does not possess exhaustive knowledge of the technical array. Granting this, before production proceeds, the producer must solve a lower-order decision problem. He must, in fact, choose among the array of extant, competing technical options. Indeed, he must, in principle, consider the possibility of technological innovation, an option which may expand the set of available options (Furubotn and Richter 1997, p. 456).

The difficulty here is apparent. The producer must decide *how to choose* among the technical options. Unfortunately, this lower-order problem contemplates both positive decision costs *and* an infinite regress problem. In principle, one must account for the decision process that resulted in employment of a particular decision rule. Granting this, one might then ask how was the prior decision process chosen, and so on. The resultant infinite regress problem has a logical corollary:

> decision costs act to limit the extent to which rationality can be displaced to higher levels. There must come a point where, as Knight says, the 'rational thing to do is to be irrational' and simply choose a choice method without reason. Otherwise, all resources would be used in decision-making (Pingle 1992, p. 11).

While the choice method may contemplate random choice, imitation, obeying authority or convention (Pingle 1992, p. 8; Conlisk 1996; Leibenstein 1985, pp. 5–8), the essential point is that there can be no presumption that the technical option chosen is 'efficient' or output maximizing. Moreover, there can be no presumption that firms in the same industry will employ the same production function.

These considerations – along with others discussed in Chapter 6 – militate against the specification of the production possibility frontier and, *mutatis mutandis*, the efficiency frontier. Indeed, the logic of the production-theoretic argument developed above calls to mind the generic point made by Lipsey and Lancaster:

> It is of the nature of the economic process...that optimization takes place at successive levels, and the maximization of a welfare function subject to a transformation function is only the topmost of these. It is also of the nature of Paretian optima...that the optimization at the different levels can be considered as independent problems (1956, p. 31).

The essential point is that, in the presence of bounded rationality and positive transaction (decision) costs, the logic of a lower-level problem – the specification of a production possibility frontier – is disturbed. Because the choice of production technique problem implicates a decision cost economizing procedure, the entrepreneur is unable to compare his actual choice with the hypothetical 'ideal' or output maximizing technical option. If he does not 'know' the efficient or output maximizing technical option he cannot make the corrections necessary to reach the 'ideal' technical configuration.

It is clear that, once allowance is made for bounded rationality, the hypothetical allocative efficiency presumed by social welfare theory cannot be achieved. While the orthodox marginal equivalences can be used to solve higher-level problems once a production technique is *somehow* chosen (Roth 1979), there can be no presumption that the production technique actually chosen is output maximizing. It follows that comparison of an observable outcome with an unachievable standard is unavailing. This has immediate implications, *inter alia*, for government policy:

> The view that now pervades much public policy economics implicitly presents the relevant choice as between an ideal norm and an existing 'imperfect' institutional arrangement...those who adopt [this] nirvana viewpoint seek to discover discrep-

ancies between the ideal and the real and, if discrepancies are found, they deduce that the real is inefficient (Demsetz 1969, p. 1).

To adopt the 'nirvana' approach is, in effect, to fail to take account of real and unavoidable constraints. Yet, this is precisely the approach adopted in the analysis of 'monopoly elements'. Departures from the Paretian ideal – as measured, for example, by the Lerner index – are regarded as *prima facie* evidence of 'monopoly power' rather than as a reflection of the 'frictions' which define real world decision environments.

In summary, it is clear that the presence of market failures – whether in the form of generalized externalities, public goods or monopoly elements – does not imply that the government can do better. The essential point is that political action, like market activity, is associated with externalities. Moreover, informational requirements are daunting. In the case of generalized externalities, the specification of single-valued marginal social and private cost curves is complicated by the fact that, generally, marginal adjustments over quantities of the 'good' are not possible, and subjectively determined, choice-influencing private costs may include quasi-rents and an imputation of the costs imposed on others. In these circumstances, determination of the 'Pareto optimal' tax or subsidy is a practical impossibility. In the case of genuinely public goods efficiency requires that each individual demander face a tax-price which reflects his marginal benefit. Yet, given the practical difficulties associated with the specification of the individual demand functions and the incentive structures of self-interested politicians, appeal to the principle of incremental benefit is, to quote Buchanan, 'politically unimaginable in modern democracy'. In the event, the resulting political externality must be weighed against the apparent market failure.

Finally, government remedies for monopoly elements – indeed for all market failures – are predicated on the deployment of a static-efficiency criterion. *Inter alia*, the standard ignores the intervention of learning, intertemporal shifts of demand curves and endogenously generated technological change. Moreover, if account is taken of bounded rationality and positive decision costs, the logic of the efficiency frontier is disturbed. The point here is not, as the general theory of second best suggests, that there is no *a priori* way to judge as between situations in which some of the Paretian-optimum conditions are fulfilled and others are not. The point is that the efficiency frontier is indeterminate. It follows that comparisons of observed outcomes with an undefined and, *pari passu*, unattainable evaluative norm is unavailing.

Granting all of this, it seems clear that normative deployment of the efficiency standard in the face of market failure cannot proceed on the assumption that 'government can do better'. If, as James Buchanan suggests, economists 'cannot resist the ever-present temptation to propose yet more complex gimmicks and gadgets for producing greater "efficiency"', they do so at considerable risk. While economists cannot be sure that the government can do better, the logic of the efficiency standard can, nevertheless, be deployed to rationalize all manner of government interventions.[6] While such interventions may be justified on other grounds, they surely cannot be justified by appeal to an indeterminate normative standard.[7]

## 5.3 THE SECOND FUNDAMENTAL WELFARE THEOREM, THE COMPENSATION PRINCIPLE, AND DISTRIBUTION ISSUES

Until now, attention has centered on the application of the efficiency standard; of the first fundamental welfare theorem. As we have seen, the second fundamental welfare theorem may be deployed to rationalize government redistribution programs (§ 4.2). While Stiglitz has suggested that, 'In assessing alternative policies, economists have put particular emphasis on economic efficiency' (1988, p. 112), much theoretical discussion has centered, implicitly, on the second fundamental theorem.

Recall first that, on the logic of social welfare theory, 'equity' or distributional issues require appeal both to the efficiency frontier and to a social welfare function (§§ 2.2 and 4.2). On this account, satisfaction of the three marginal equivalences – or 'welfare conditions' – assures only that a first-best Paretian optimum will be attained somewhere on the efficiency frontier. Whether this 'competitive equilibrium' is also the 'socially desired' or 'ethical equilibrium' depends on whether a social indifference curve is tangent at that point.[8] In the event that a tangency does not obtain, a reconciliation of the two equilibria can be achieved by appeal to a system of lump-sum taxes and bounties.

The literature which addresses these issues falls generally under the rubric of public finance (Viscusi, Vernon and Harrington 2000, p. 75). The work of Harvey Rosen (1999) is heuristic. According to him, 'Rationales for Income Redistribution' depend upon the properties imputed to the social welfare function: 'In the utilitarian framework, the form of the social welfare function plays a crucial role in determining the appropriate governmental redistribution policy' (Rosen 1999, p. 150).[9]

Particular interest centers on the additive social welfare function and on what is characterized as a Rawlsian social welfare function.[10] Whereas the former regards 'social welfare' as the simple sum of individuals' utilities, the latter deploys a maximin criterion. In effect, the 'social objective' is to maximize the utility of the person with the lowest utility.

On the assumptions, (1) that individuals have *identical* utility functions that depend only on individuals' incomes, (2) that individual utility functions exhibit diminishing marginal utility of income, and (3) that total income is fixed, the additive social welfare function implies 'that government should redistribute income so as to achieve complete equality' (Rosen 1999, p. 148). For its part, the 'Rawlsian' social welfare function 'implies that the income distribution should be perfectly equal, *except* to the extent that departures from equality increase the welfare of the worst-off person' (1999, p. 151).

While the literature also contemplates a consequentialist-procedural approach which emphasizes equality of 'capabilities' this construal has already been evaluated (§ 2.23).[11] What, then, can be said about the purely consequentialist 'additive' social welfare function, and about the so-called 'Rawlsian' social welfare function?

Consider first the view that Rawlsian justice can be reduced to a consequentialist social welfare function. Reduced to its essentials, the difficulty here is that the Rawlsian maximin criterion is not consequentialist. On Rawls's account, the criterion emerges as a result of impartial deliberation among morally equivalent persons who employ a contract device – the veil of ignorance – to derive rules of justice (§§ 1.5 and 2.22). Whether such deliberation would result in the emergence of the maximin criterion is open to question. This question is, however, beside the point. Neither the view that persons are morally equivalent, nor respect for rights, nor the duty to promote just institutions is reconcilable with social welfare theory (§ 2.3). It follows that, effectively, there is no such thing as a 'Rawlsian' social welfare function.

Consider now the additive social welfare function. As Rosen acknowledges, the generative assumptions which determine the properties of the function are open to question (1999, pp. 149–150). Particularly troublesome are the assumptions that individuals have identical utility functions, and that society's total income is fixed. That said, there are more fundamental problems.

As we have seen, it is possible to question the existence of a social welfare function. Sen's attempts to expand the informational base of social welfare theory notwithstanding (§ 2.23), both the impossibility of the Paretian liberal (§ 2.1) and Arrow's Possibility Result (§ 2.2) militate against the *specification* of a social welfare function. Moreover, as we have seen, it is possible to raise a 'quite persuasive' ontological objection to the *idea* of a social welfare function (§ 3.2). If nothing else were said, it should be clear that the 'socially desired' or 'ethical' equilibrium is indeterminate. Granting this, it is impossible to determine what 'optimal redistribution' policy should be deployed.

More can, however, be said. As has been emphasized, right-based (§ 2.2), contractarian (§§ 2.21 and 2.22) and consequentialist-procedural (§ 2.23) theories of justice cannot be accommodated by social welfare theory. Moreover, the implicit 'time-slice' theory of justice to which social welfare theory gives rise is open to serious question (§ 2.24). *Inter alia*, nothing in the theory allows for the moral appraisal either of the initial endowment from which the 'competitive equilibrium' derives or the *process* employed to affect any 'socially desired' redistribution.[12]

Given both the logical, empirical and ontological problems associated with the social welfare function and the absence of an acceptable theory of justice, government redistribution policies 'justified' by social welfare theory must be regarded as *ad hoc*. James Buchanan has summarized the situation in this way:

> The [social welfare] function orders all possible social situations and allows an external observer to select one as 'best'. Presumably, this 'best' point will be on the 'welfare frontier'.... Individual preferences, insofar as they enter the constru-tion...must be those which *appear to the observer* rather than those revealed by the behavior of the individuals themselves. In other words,...these preferences must be those presumed by the observer rather than those revealed in behavior....
>
> The function may be useful as a device in assisting the decision-making of a despot, benevolent or otherwise, an organic state, or a single-minded ruling group. But, once this limitation is recognized, individual preferences, even as presumed by the observer, need not enter the construction at all except insofar as it becomes necessary to consider predicted individual reaction to coercively imposed changes. The Pareto conception of 'optimality' loses most of its significance ([1959] 1999, p. 203).

The essential point is that, in the standard formulation, the omniscient economist-observer (Graaff 1957, p. 13) is presumed to advise a benevolent despot (§4.4). That the observer cannot 'know' the disparate desiderata of individual, autonomous agents is clear (Chapter 6). That the benevolent despot formulation unrealistically suppresses narrowly construed self-interest is also clear. In the event, both because the observer can only presume to know the relevant preference (and value) structures, and because any 'index of group welfare must inevitably make normative judgments in which the gains to some are weighed against the losses of others', it is plausible to argue that, in fact, 'measures of group welfare used by practitioners have been developed in an *ad hoc* manner with little or no welfare economic justification' (Slesnick 1998, p. 2137).

While I regard the *ad hoc* nature of group welfare measures – and, *pari passu*, of government redistribution programs – as the predictable consequence of the indeterminancy of both the social welfare function and the efficiency frontier, the essential point is that the growth of government cannot be justified by appeal to the first and second fundamental welfare theorems. This admittedly circumspect view extends to the deployment of the 'compensation principle' and to the distinction between actual and potential increases in welfare. *Inter alia*, applications of the Kaldor-Hicks-Scitovsky-Samuelson approach to compensation mechanisms contemplate *possible* lump-sum redistributions of goods across the population. The presumption is that

> the appropriate criterion for evaluating [government] policies is whether the dollar value of the policy change to those who benefit from it exceeds the dollar value of the loss to those who are made worse off. In these circumstances, the gainers could, in principle, compensate the losers. This principle is referred to as the compensation principle. It makes the implicit assumption that a dollar's worth of gain to one individual should be weighted the same as a dollar's worth of loss to another (Stiglitz 1988, pp. 100–101).

While much can be said about this, it is sufficient to emphasize four points. First, appeal to the compensation principle requires, *inter alia*, that, in the manner suggested by Hicks (1939, p. 31), real income be regarded as equivalent to utility. That this presumption, while analytically convenient, is questionable should be obvious (Hausman and McPherson 1993, pp. 689–693). Second, the implicit assumption that a dollar gained by one individual should be weighted the same as a dollar lost by another individual requires that individuals' preferences be identical and homothetic (Slesnick 1998, p. 2140). That this is implausible should also be obvious (Chapter 6). Third, even if these problems are not acknowledged, there are practical difficulties. As Stiglitz has emphasized, 'The compensations that would enable some policy change to be a Pareto improvement frequently are not made because it is often difficult to identify either the gainers and losers or the magnitude of their gains and losses' (1988, p. 101). Moreover, putting aside the problem that 'lump-sum measures are extraordinarily hard to devise' (Graaff 1957, p. 78), it is 'not feasible to examine all possible lump-sum redistributions of goods across the population under each scenario' (Slesnick 1998, p. 2140).[13] Finally, as has been emphasized, social welfare theory does not deploy an explicit theory of justice. While the theory incorporates an implicit 'time-slice' theory of justice (§ 2.24), the latter does not constitute 'the whole story about distributive shares' (Nozick 1974, p. 154). The essential point is that social welfare theory cannot provide a *moral* justification for redistribution programs motivated by the compensation principle.[14]

The upshot of all of this is that, whereas welfare economists have relied upon the first and second welfare theorems to provide 'a rationale for political interferences' (Buchanan [1990] 1999, p. 185), logical, empirical and ethical problems suggest that they should not be used for this purpose. On the one hand, the theory can be used to rationalize public (and private) sector corruption (§ 5.1). On the other hand, the analysis of 'market failure' proceeds, *inter alia*, on the presumption that the 'government can do better'

(§ 5.2). While this is problematic, the fundamental problem is that the efficiency standard is indeterminate (Chapter 6). Finally, appeal to the second fundamental welfare theorem has facilitated the rationalization of government redistribution programs. As we have seen, appeal to a social welfare function or to the 'compensation principle' is unavailing. While serious questions attach to the specification – indeed to the existence – of the former, the latter is encumbered by empirical and other difficulties. More fundamentally, because it does not incorporate an acceptable theory of justice, the second fundamental welfare theorem cannot provide a moral justification for government redistribution programs.

The fact that neither welfare theorem is suitable for public policy appraisal is underscored by the fact that consequentialist social welfare theory lacks a theory of government (§ 4.4). Transparently, the 'benevolent despot' model implicit in the theory cannot be reconciled with objective features of observable reality. On the one hand, 'government' is not subsumed by the notion of a single (benevolent) decision-maker. On the other hand, the notion of a 'bifurcated man' who is narrowly self-interested in his market behavior but 'noble' in his political activity strains credulity. Plainly, the 'political process' is characterized by the interaction of boundedly rational principals (voters) and agents (elected representatives and 'bureaucrats'). Whatever else is said, the observable decision environment is characterized by information asymmetry and opportunism.

It is this decision environment – rather than the 'frictionless' one assumed by social welfare theory (§ 4.2) – in which the logic of the two welfare theorems is deployed. It is, in short, an environment which is congenial to political rent seeking. With respect to the first fundamental welfare theorem, it has been said that

> If…governmental action moves significantly beyond the limits defined by the minimal or protective state, if government commences, as it has done on a sweeping scale, to interfere piece-meal in the market adjustment process, the tendency toward the erosion or dissipation of rents is countered and may be wholly blocked. Rents must remain, however, and the signals emitted to potential competitors remain as strong as they are under standard market adjustment. Hence, attempts will be made to capture these rents…. Rent-seeking activity is directly related to the scope and range of governmental activity in the economy, to the relative size of the public sector (Buchanan [1980] 1999, pp. 108–109).

In effect, government interventions motivated by perceived 'market failures' are the catalyst to rent seeking activity which, in turn, may further expand the scope and range of government activity. If 'efficiency-enhancing' policies contemplating generalized externalities, public goods and 'monopoly elements' present rent seeking opportunities, so too do tax, trade, and other policies motivated by 'efficiency' and 'social purpose' considerations (Chapter 9).

If rent seeking is associated with government market interventions motivated by the first fundamental welfare theorem, the same can be said of the second theorem. As has been emphasized, social welfare theory can accommodate neither right-based, nor contractarian or consequentialist-procedural understandings of justice (Chapter 2). Moreover, the 'time-slice' theory of justice implicit in the theory leaves many distributional questions unanswered (§ 2.24). It follows that government redistribution policies informed by the second fundamental welfare theorem may be characterized as *ad hoc*. As Stiglitz has suggested, 'The most severe limitation of the Pareto principle is that it provides no guidance concerning issues of income distribution. Most government programs (when their costs are taken into account) benefit some individuals at the expense of others' (1998, p. 94). I do not disagree. I would add, however, that the same might be said of redistribution programs motivated either by appeal to a 'social welfare function' or to the 'compensation principle'. Both the prospect of the initiation of, and the existence of, such programs provide incentive for rent seeking activities and, *pari passu*, for an expansion of the scope and range of government activities.

## NOTES

1. Interestingly, Acemoglu and Verdier (2000) employ a model of 'government as a benevolent social planner' to argue that 'second-best government intervention may involve a certain fraction of bureaucrats accepting bribes'. For his part, Garoupa (2000) has suggested that, under certain conditions, extortion may be 'social welfare improving'.
2. Again, see Scruton (1994, p. 283).
3. Other devices may be employed to bring about the internalization of social costs. However, whether 'the government' appeals to effluent fees, direct regulation or some other institutional arrangement, the objective is to bring internalized costs into conformity with social costs.
4. See Roth (1979) for an application of these concepts to the case of publicly generated and disseminated information. In the situation envisioned, a different marginal tax price would, in principle, be charged to different demanders. Thus, Ford Motor Company may, in principle, be charged a different price than, say, General Motors. Whatever else is said, this may be good economics but bad politics.
5. Lizzeri and Persico (2001, p. 237) have argued that 'When [political] candidates have the option of redistributing resources, public goods will be underprovided relative to the efficient outcome'. The logic from which this conclusion derives is that, from the perspective of self-interested politicians, 'benefits from the public good cannot be targeted to groups of voters as easily as the benefits from pork barrel projects or pure transfers' (pp. 237–238).
6. In one account, 'Expenditures incurred because of federal environmental, health, and safety regulations have grown dramatically in recent decades, and now total several hundred billion dollars annually' (Hahn 1998, p. 201).
7. Stiglitz (1988, p. 83) has suggested that, whereas the efficiency standard 'has caused many programs to be justified in terms of market failures...this may simply be rhetoric':

> There is often a significant difference between the stated objective of a program (to remedy market failure) and the design of the program. Political rhetoric may focus on the failure of markets to provide insurance against volatile prices and the consequences that this has on small farmers, but government agricultural programs may in practice transfer income to large farmers.

This 'demand for regulation' is a reflection of private sector rent seeking behavior. For more on this, see § 8.1.

8. For more on this, see Stiglitz (1988, pp. 98–99).
9. See also Stiglitz (1988, pp. 104–112).
10. See, for example, Slesnick (1998, pp. 2149–2150).
11. Procedural approaches to justice and, *pari passu*, to distributional issues are not reconcilable with consequentialist social welfare theory. See §§ 2.21 and 2.22 and Chapter 7.
12. Indeed, some account is taken of this in the literature. See, for example, Rosen (1999, pp. 153–154).
13. See also Sen (1979) and Stiglitz (1988, pp. 101–102).
14. See also Buchanan ([1959] 1999, p. 193) and Stiglitz (1988, p. 101).

# 6. The indeterminacy of social welfare theory

## 6.1 A REPRISE

As has been repeatedly emphasized, the 'new' social welfare theory deploys two fundamental analytical constructs. Broadly speaking, the efficiency or welfare frontier may be regarded as summarizing the system of constraints operative at a cross-section of time, while the utilitarian social welfare function constitutes the objective function.

While all points on the efficiency frontier satisfy the three marginal equivalences or 'efficiency' conditions, only one of these first-best Paretian optima constitutes the 'competitive equilibrium' to which a perfectly competitive system is impelled.[1] A competitive equilibrium may or may not be an 'ethical equilibrium'. The latter is determined at the point of tangency of a social indifference curve and the efficiency frontier. Finally, a reconciliation of the competitive and ethical equilibria can, in principle, be accomplished by appeal to a system of lump-sum taxes and bounties.

While earlier chapters have raised fundamental questions about the new social welfare theory paradigm, immediate interest centers on the *existence* of the efficiency frontier.

## 6.2 THE FRICTIONLESS NEOCLASSICAL DECISION ENVIRONMENT

As is well known, the logic of the efficiency frontier requires that the under lying utility and production functions possess orthodox, neoclassical properties, and that the decision environment be 'frictionless' (§ 4.2).[2]

Let us first stipulate that the properties imputed to functional relationships are embodied in sets of statements – generative assumptions – which serve to generate hypotheses, given certain auxiliary assumptions (Melitz 1965). From the positivist or instrumentalist perspective, this distinction is crucial: Whereas generative assumptions need not be realistic,[3] the empirical confirmability (discomfirmability) of an hypothesis depends upon the realism of auxiliary assumptions. Given the realism of a model's auxiliary assumptions, tests of the model center on the correspondence of predictions with observable reality (Keita 1992; Roth 1998).

With this as background, *homo economicus* is central to the neoclassical paradigm. *Homo economicus* is taken to be an autonomous, atomistic decision maker who seeks purposefully to maximize utility subject to one or more exogenously determined constraints. The key property of his utility function is captured by classical rationality, a generative assumption. On this account, the decision maker's preference structure is consistently ordered, exogenously determined and stable. With stability of preferences understood to be an auxiliary assumption, the presumption is that the classically rational decision maker acts in his narrow self-interest (Persky 1995, p. 223). For their part, the desiderata, the objects of choice, are taken to be purchasable economic goods whose properties – both physical and technical – are known with certainty, and whose associated property rights are well-defined and unattenuated. Finally, in this 'frictionless' decision environment, information asymmetries and opportunistic behavior are absent and, *pari passu*, ethical norms play no role.

Granting all of this, there is a one-to-one correspondence between economic man's objective and subjectively perceived environments. In the situation envisioned, because fully informed decision makers affect instantaneous exchange, transaction costs and, *pari passu*, the *ex ante* and *ex post* costs of contract enforcement are zero.

While much can be said about this characterization of economic man's decision environment, immediate interest centers on the classical rationality postulate.[4]

First, as seems increasingly to be appreciated, the classical rationality postulate cannot be tested independently of stability of preferences (Robinson 1962). It follows, *pari passu*, that tests of its predictions are neither confirmatory nor disconfirmatory of the model (Roth 1998, Chapter 1). While the literature characterizes the problem as reflecting the presence of an unidentified exogenous variable (Roth 1998, p. 9), this is fundamentally misleading. In fact, preference structures are endogenously determined (Buchanan 1994b, pp. 76–77). Broadly speaking, evolutionary[5] and other path dependencies including learning, the development of social norms[6] and the emergence of new products influence preference and value structures.[7] These path dependencies may, in turn, account for the 'anomalous behavior' judged to be inconsistent with classical rationality (Tversky and Thaler 1990). In effect, such behavior may reflect learning, the intervention of social norms, experience and, perhaps, higher-order preferences (North 1994). It seems clear, for example, that some persons have 'preferences for preferences', and that they seek to alter others' preference structures (Buchanan 1994b, pp. 74–77). Equally important, decision processes may be characterized by 'internal conflict'; by concern for others, and for persons' perceptions of each other

(Hausman and McPherson 1993, p. 688). *Inter alia*, this suggests that ethical and other behavioural norms may appear as arguments of utility functions and/or as constraints on behavior (Buchanan 1994a, pp. 128 and 133).[8]

If these considerations call into question the exogeneity and intertemporal stability of preferences, it is also possible to question the empirical content of the classical rationality postulate.[9] In Herbert Simon's view, there is a discrepancy

> between the perfect rationality that is assumed in classical and neoclassical economic theory and the reality of human behavior.... The point [is] not that people are consciously and deliberately irrational...but that neither their knowledge nor their powers of calculation allow them to achieve the high level of optimal adaptation of means to ends that is posited in economics (1992, p. 3).[10]

Whereas for economic man 'there is no gap between an agent's competence and the difficulty of the decision problem to be solved' (Heiner 1983, p. 562), cognitive limitations are the defining characteristic of the boundedly rational decision maker (Conlisk 1996).[11] While there is no generally accepted definition of bounded rationality (Furubotn and Richter 1997, p. 39), there is general agreement that it implies what has been characterized as a competence-difficulty (C–D) Gap. Accordingly, optimization is 'a special case occurring when uncertainty (the C–D gap) approaches zero' (Wilde, LeBaron and Israelsen 1985, p. 403).

If one grants that decision makers are boundedly rational, certain corollaries follow. *Inter alia*, individuals differ with respect to the stocks of knowledge they possess, their ability to process extant and incremental knowledge, and their ability to distinguish between the effects of random events generated by the environment and those which result from opportunistic behavior (Williamson 1985, p. 47). If the confluence of cognitive limitations, random events and opportunism implies that 'completely accurate monitoring and full enforcement of property rights are impossible' (Furubotn 1994, p. 25), it also suggests that an economic case can be made for an explicit accounting of the role and importance of ethical norms. Whereas the logic of consequentialist social welfare theory can accommodate the notion of 'efficiency-enhancing' corruption (§ 5.1), the logic of bounded rationality underscores the importance of ethical behavior. At issue is not simply the reduction of transaction costs which ethically constrained behavior implies. More fundamentally, respect for rights and their correlative duties plays an instrumental role in the functioning of impersonal markets (Furubotn and Richter 1997, p. 140).[12] Yet, as we have seen, consequentialist social welfare theory cannot accommodate the moral force of the rights which are instrumentally important to the achievement of first-best Paretian optima (§ 2.1). Granting this – and given the importance of ethical behavior to the functioning of markets – intendedly value-free social welfare theory must give way to a theory which acknowledges the endogeneity of preference and value structures.[13] Indeed, economic theory must acknowledge the reciprocal nature of preference and value structures and the setting within which such structures are shaped: 'The methodological individualist must...acknowledge the relationships between individual utility functions and the socioeconomic–legal–political–cultural setting within which evaluations are made' (Buchanan 1991, p. 186).[14]

While the 'positivist revolution' may have displaced it, this view of man has a long history in economics. Indeed, Adam Smith, 'the founder of modern economics' (Tribe 1999, p. 609) argued that

> How selfish soever man may be supposed, there are evidently some principles in his nature, which interest him in the fortunes of others, and render their happiness necessary to him, though he derives nothing from it except the pleasure of seeing it. Of this kind is pity or compassion.... (Smith [1759] 1976, p. 9).

> Sympathy...enlivens joy and alleviates grief. It enlivens joy by presenting another source of satisfaction; and it alleviates grief by insinuating into the heart almost the only agreeable sensation which it is at the time capable of receiving (Smith [1759] 1976, p. 14).[15]

If Adam Smith's view of what may be characterized as multiple preference domains is more than three centuries old, empirical findings in evolutionary psychology comport with his thinking.[16] There is evidence, for example, that 'One or more of [a] collection of distinct [cognitive] processing units weighs or tries to weigh economic goods according to the laws of transitivity, but other processes register utility in at least five other ways' (Aaron 1994, p. 15). In effect, utility derives from the consumption of comestibles. But it also derives from self-reference, from helping and hurting others, from caring about others as 'ends', from interpersonal relationships, and from setting goals and achieving them.

It should be clear that path-dependent, multiple preference domains cannot be represented by a single-equation, intertemporally stable and exogenously determined utility function. While discussion of the solution to this problem is deferred until § 6.3, it is sufficient for the moment to emphasize that economic man's motivation is too narrowly construed. Indeed, these and other considerations led Amartya Sen to suggest that

> There is a lot to be done.... Quite a lot of high-brow economics...accepts the appropriateness of the standard general equilibrium model, with everyone pursuing their self-interest, given taste and technology.... But the high ground is not secure at all. The most basic element of such modeling, namely the motivation of human beings, is not well addressed (Klamer 1989, p. 147).[17]

Economic man's single-equation utility function has an analog in neoclassical production theory. At the heart of the formulation is the assumption that production proceeds under the technical restrictions imposed by a single-equation, flow–flow production function. *Inter alia*, the function is presumed to be the only 'efficient' or output-maximizing technical alternative available. Moreover, in its short-run configuration the production function reflects 'perfect adaptability'. In effect, the logic of the 'efficiency' assumption requires that, as movement along the short-run expansion path proceeds, the physical form of the capital stock which generates the fixed service flow must be instantaneously and costlessly adapted to changing rates of use of the variable service flow (Furubotn 1964, p. 22).[18] In the situation envisioned, while the service flow, $x_2^0$, is 'fixed', each point on the short-run expansion path is associated with a unique, differentiated form of the capital input type, $K_2$.

What seems not to be acknowledged is that, as the physical form of a capital input type changes, the technical properties of the 'fixed' service flow change. It follows that, as adaptation proceeds, the production function changes and movement along the short-run expansion path is a logical impossibility (Roth 1974).

The perfect adaptability conundrum has basic relevance to social welfare theory. The essential idea is that fundamental engineering considerations militate against the specification of a single 'efficient' production function. We know that, at a cross-section of time, capital input types – whether human or nonhuman – appear in technologically distinct, differentiated forms. This, in turn, has implications for the firm's 'technology'.

Reduced to its essentials, the firm's production function is properly characterized as a multi-equation construct. While each of the production subfunctions is capable of producing the product in question, each has as its parameters the particular differentiates of the capital input types employed.

Given this understanding of the firm's technical environment, the entrepreneur confronts a 'choice of technique' problem: Whatever his desideratum, he must somehow choose among the competing production subfunctions or 'techniques' (Roth 1972; 1977).

As we have seen, the choice of production technique problem is complicated by the intervention of bounded rationality and positive transaction (decision) costs (§ 5.2). It is characteristic of the process that the entrepreneur must decide *how* to choose. Granting this, whatever decision rule is selected, it is plausible to ask how it was selected. Yet the decision process which resulted in the emergence of the decision rule was, itself, the outcome of a prior decision process. The resulting infinite regress problem implies that 'the rational thing to do is to be irrational', and simply 'to choose a choice method without reason' (Pingle 1992, p. 11).

The plausibility of a decision to 'choose a choice method without reason' is enhanced once account is taken of two additional features of observable reality. First, the number of production subfunctions confronting the entrepreneur depends both upon the number of capital input types employed, and upon the number of differentiates of each of the capital input types. It follows, *pari passu*, that in many cases of practical importance, the entrepreneur cannot have exhaustive knowledge of the technical array. Second, allowance must be made for the possibility of technical interaction (Gort and Boddy 1965, p. 395). There are, in brief, 'strong logical and empirical grounds for believing direct linkages exist among the units forming a production complex' (Furubotn 1970, p. 22). Once allowance is made for extant and potential technical interactions, the effect is to expand the number of definable – and competing – production subfunctions or techniques.

The practical effect of these considerations is clear. Serious questions emerge as to whether the extent of the array, let alone the technical characteristics of each of the production subfunctions, is knowable. Given bounded rationality and positive decision costs,

> it is no longer possible to assume that each individual knows everything about existing technological alternatives.... The older formalism of the neoclassical case does not apply when individual knowledge endowments are limited, differ widely from person to person, and are subject to continuing change, and when the very process of decision making is costly and based on decision rules other than rational choice (Furubotn 1999, p. 183).

According to this there will be a divergence between the objective – but unknowable – decision environment, and its subjectively perceived counterpart.[19] In effect, the complexity of the choice of technique problem suggests that the entrepreneur does not possess exhaustive knowledge of the available technical options and that, *pari passu*, only a subset of the options will be considered.[20] It follows that there can be no presumption that incumbent firms or *de novo* industry entrants will employ the same differentiates of the capital input types typically employed within an industry. Moreover, given that differentiated forms of capital input types generate technologically distinct service flows it follows that the service flows employed across firms in the same industry need not be technologically homogeneous. Yet, if this is true within industries, it must, *mutatis mutandis*, be true across industries.

Whatever else is said, the logic of the firm-subjective production function is not reconcilable with the production-theoretic foundations of social welfare theory. The essential difficulty is that, given bounded rationality and positive decision costs, there can be no presumption that all firms will employ the same production function – let alone the same service flows. Granting this, the space in which the contract curve might be defined is indeterminate.

It follows, *pari passu*, that the production possibility frontier – a *sine qua non* for the derivation of the efficiency frontier – cannot be defined.

## 6.3 THE IMPLICATIONS FOR THE EFFICIENCY FRONTIER

Fundamental features of observable reality militate against the specification of the efficiency frontier. Generation of the frontier is predicated, in part, upon the existence of the production possibility frontier. Yet the logic of the production possibility frontier requires, *inter alia*, that all producers, both within and across industries, employ the same productive service flows. As we have seen, this analytically convenient assumption is irreconcilable with a technical environment characterized by cognitive limitations, information asymmetries and positive decision costs. Reduced to its essentials, the employment of subjectively determined production functions and technologically heterogeneous service flows is inconsistent with the derivation of the production possibility frontier. This, in turn, means that it is not possible to effect a mapping of utility possibility frontiers and, *pari passu*, the efficiency frontier. In effect, the subjectivity of the underlying production functions renders the efficiency frontier indeterminate.

If the production-theoretic foundations of the efficiency frontier may be called into question, the same is true of its utility-theoretic underpinnings. As we saw in Section 6.2, the individual's preference and value structure cannot adequately be represented by an intertemporally stable, single-equation utility function. On the one hand, path dependencies are a palpable reality. Their existence rules out the admittedly analytically convenient presumption that preference and value structures are both constant and exogenously determined. On the other hand, an emerging literature suggests that individual preference systems involve a number of preference domains (§ 6.2). Each of these preference domains is representable by a utility subfunction defined for the same individual. While the arguments of a number of these subfunctions include comestibles, the presumption must be that one or more of the subfunctions contemplates arguments which are broadly reflective of society's view of acceptable behavior. In effect, the individual's utility domains incorporate both tastes and values or moral tastes. According to this logic, 'the attempted separation between economics and morals was, at best, an illusion that simply cannot be sustained. Economics models persons as maximizers of utility, but arguments in utility functions include rules that restrict the range of choices that are made' (Buchanan 1944a, p. 128).

While much can be said about this, the essential point is that an explicit accounting of utility domains requires appeal to a multi-equation utility function construct. This, in turn, compromises the familiar logic of contract curve derivation. Even if it were assumed that individuals' preference and value structures are defined over the same utility domains, the space in which contract curves might be derived is indeterminate. In any case, the implausibility of such an assumption is clear. The interaction of bounded rationality, information asymmetries and path dependencies would seem to ensure that individuals will be characterized by disparate preference and value domains. Granting this, the arguments of individuals' utility subfunctions will differ, and the contract curves which are a *sine qua non* for the derivation of the efficiency frontier are indeterminate.

The indeterminacy of the efficiency frontier is reinforced once account is taken of the complex nature of individuals' desiderata. The problem is not simply that individuals' preference and value domains are not homogeneous. The core problem is that product types typically appear in differentiated forms. Indeed, the array of goods extant at a cross-section of time may be distinguished by their technical and aesthetic characteristics, by their associated property rights bundles and by their ethical attributes (both in use and in acquisition) (Buchanan 1994a, p. 134; Furubotn and Pejovich 1974; Roth 1975). In effect, each differentiate of each product type is characterized by a vector of characteristics, some of which are subjectively perceived. It follows, *pari passu*, that there can be no reasonable presumption that, for any two individuals, the 'goods' appearing as arguments in their respective utility subfunctions will be the same. There can, in fact, be no presumption that a boundedly rational individual knows the number, let alone the objectively determinable characteristics, of the goods and services which confront him. Granting this, the goods which appear in each individual's utility subfunctions must consist in a subjectively determined subset of the extant array of comestibles. Add to this the intertemporal emergence of new product types, and of new differentiates of existing product types, and there can be no one-to-one correspondence between the objectively defined and subjectively perceived decision environments. Finally, given that boundedly rational individuals are possessed of differing stocks of knowledge, have differing abilities to process extant and new information, and are conditioned by differing path-dependent phenomena, it follows that subjectively perceived decision environments must differ among individuals. A corollary is that both at a cross-section of time and intertemporally individuals will be possessed of heterogeneous objective functions. In effect, each individual's multi-equation utility function will be defined on disparate preference and value domains, and on differing, subjectively perceived subsets of the available comestibles.

Granting the logic of what has been said, it is clear that the 'goods' space in which contract curves might be derived is indeterminate. It follows, *pari passu*, that the efficiency frontier cannot be derived.

At issue here is not the oft-cited nirvana fallacy. Whereas the fallacy obtains when the efficiency frontier is deployed as a benchmark without taking explicit account of real and unavoidable constraints (§ 5.2), the problem outlined here is more fundamental. The observable features of complex reality suggest that the efficiency frontier cannot meaningfully be defined. Stated differently, it is appropriate to call into question the ontological existence of the efficiency frontier (Frank 1996, p. 119; Furubotn 1994).

## 6.4 RIGHTS, ZERO TRANSACTION COSTS AND THE PATH TO THE EFFICIENCY FRONTIER

It should be clear that the indeterminacy or, more properly, the nonexistence of the efficiency frontier has implications for government policies informed by the first and second fundamental welfare theorems (§ 4.3). While those implications are the subject matter of Section 6.6, let us suppose for the moment that the efficiency frontier *can* be defined meaningfully. As it happens, even if the existence of the frontier were granted, fundamental, logical problems remain. In particular, contrary to the received view, the path to first-best Paretian optima is not assured.

To see this, recall first that consequentialist social welfare theory is a hybrid moral theory (§ 2.1). While the theory is outcomes-based and procedurally-detached, it nevertheless assigns an instrumental role to unattenuated property and exchange rights. In particular, the path to first-best Paretian optima – the 'competitive equilibria' defined on the efficiency frontier – is reliant upon respect for individual agents' property and exchange rights. Difficulties arise precisely because social welfare theory is formulated in utilitarian terms. Reduced to its essentials, the problem is that utility considerations trump rights. As Lyons has emphasized, 'evaluation of conduct from a utilitarian standpoint is dominated by direct utilitarian arguments and therefore ignores the moral force of justified legal rights' (1982, p. 113).

The essential point is that utilitarian social welfare theory cannot accommodate the moral force of the rights which it regards as instrumentally important. Once this has been said, it is clear that even if one were to suppose that it exists, the path to the frontier is compromised.

If the irreconcilability of right- and goal-based moral theories jeopardizes the path to 'competitive equilibria' so too does the zero transaction cost assumption (§ 4.2). Characteristically, social welfare theorists regard costless transactions among autonomous, atomistic agents as a necessary condition for the achievement of competitive equilibria. The difficulty is that, contrary to the conventional wisdom, the zero transaction cost assumption leads to a logical conundrum. The essential idea is that a decision environment characterized by costless transactions is congenial to the formation of coalitions which, effectively, rule out the satisfaction of the conditions for a first-best Paretian optimum (Furubotn 1991). The upshot is that, even if one granted its existence, logical inconsistencies inherent in social welfare theory compromise the path to the efficiency frontier.

## 6.5 THE INDETERMINACY OF THE SOCIAL WELFARE FUNCTION

As we have repeatedly seen, the social welfare function is understood to be an interest-aggregation decision mechanism which defines the optimal social outcome as the maximization of the sum of individual utilities. It is in this sense that it is understood to be a mechanism for deciding among states-of-affairs. Because it is utilitarian, it presupposes the normative judgment that the desideratum, the standard of outcome evaluation, is that the optimal state is that which maximizes aggregate utility or 'welfare' (§ 2.1).[21] Granting this, the social welfare function is the *sine qua non* for the determination of 'ethical equilibria' (§ 2.2).

That this characterization of the 'public good' (§ 3.2) should have persisted for more than six decades is remarkable. Recall first that Arrow's Possibility Result (1951) established that, if interpersonal utility comparisons are ruled out, there is no possible method of aggregating individual rankings of social alternatives which meets five apparently innocuous criteria (§ 2.2). Difficulties arise precisely because interpersonal utility comparisons must be ruled out. The irremediable fact is that individuals' preference and value structures are both path-dependent (§ 6.2) and defined on complex utility domains (§ 6.3). Add to this the fact that there is no one-to-one correspondence between boundedly rational agents' objectively defined and subjectively perceived decision environments (§ 6.3), and it is clear that interpersonal utility comparisons are a practical impossibility.

If the interpersonal utility comparison problem militates against the specification of a social welfare function, so too does the impossibility of the Paretian liberal. Reduced to its essentials, the juxtaposition of meddlesome preferences and respect for minimal privacy rights militates against the emergence of any social choice (§ 2.1). The upshot is that, Professor Sen's efforts to expand the informational base of social welfare theory notwithstanding (§ 2.23), Arrow's Possibility Result and the impossibility of the Paretian liberal call into question the efficacy of the social welfare function as an interest-aggregation decision mechanism.

While empirical and logical questions attach to the specification of a social welfare function, a more fundamental, ontological objection has been raised

(§ 3.2). As Professor Buchanan has suggested, the idea of 'social preference' imputes 'rationality or irrationality as an attribute of the social group'. This, in turn, 'implies the imputation to that group of an organic existence apart from that of its individual components' (Buchanan 1954, p. 116). Significantly, Professor Sen finds this objective 'quite persuasive' when 'social preference' connotes the operation of social decision mechanisms such as voting procedures (1995, p. 5). When combined with the logical and empirical problems already cited, it is clear that efforts to deploy the second fundamental welfare theorem to rationalize government redistribution policies must be regarded as *ad hoc* (§ 5.3).

## 6.6 THE IMPLICATIONS FOR THE CONSEQUENTIALIST APPROACH TO GOVERNMENT

Let us first stipulate that, even if it were supposed that the efficiency frontier has an operational counterpart, fundamental problems must be faced. First, the general theory of second best 'show[s] the futility of "piecemeal welfare economics"' (Lipsey and Lancaster 1956, p. 17). Suffice it to say that, because invocations of the first fundamental welfare theorem invariably occur in a partial equilibrium context, there can be no presumption that government policy initiatives will be 'efficiency-enhancing'. Second, while most welfare theorists regard unattenuated property and exchange rights as instrumental to the achievement of first-best Paretian optima, the inability of utilitarian theory to accommodate the moral force of rights leads to a logical conundrum. Either social welfare theorists must argue that the rights which they regard as important are morally exigent in themselves and reject the efficiency standard, or they must embrace the efficiency standard and deny the moral force of rights (§ 2.1). The literature on 'efficiency-enhancing' corruption suggests that some social welfare theorists have adopted the latter approach (§ 5.1). Third, social welfare theorists appear to have forgotten that the theory is predicated upon the existence both of a benevolent despot (§ 4.4), and of an 'omniscient being – the observing economist' (§ 5.2). It should be self-evident that, while analytically convenient, both conventions strain credulity. In any case, for reasons discussed above (§§ 4.4 and 5.2), there can be no presumption that, 'if the market fails, the government is sure to do better'. Finally, the zero transaction cost assumption is congenial to the emergence of coalitions which, effectively, rule out the satisfaction of the conditions for a first-best Paretian optimum (§ 6.4).

Each of these logical and empirical problems has basic relevance even if the efficiency frontier is presumed to have an operational counterpart. That said, we have seen that objective features of observable reality militate against the specification of the frontier. Granting this, what are the implications for the social welfare theorists' theory of the state? Recall, first, that the theory is effectively summarized by the two fundamental welfare theorems (§ 4.3). Considered in order, the implications are as follows: (1) The indeterminacy of the efficiency frontier suggests that invocations of the first fundamental welfare theorem are unavailing. Stated differently, the indeterminacy of the efficiency frontier implies that the efficiency standard cannot meaningfully be deployed as a normative standard. It follows that the 'market failure' analysis standardly employed by economists should not be regarded as justificatory of government market intervention; (2) The indeterminacy of the social welfare function, when coupled with the absence of an explicit theory of justice (§ 4.3), implies that the second fundamental welfare theorem cannot justify government redistribution policies.[22] In fact, redistribution policies animated by the theorem must be regarded as *ad hoc*.

The empirical, logical and ontological difficulties outlined above suggest that social welfare theory can serve neither as a 'positive' theory of the state[23] nor as an instrument for normative public policy appraisal. Something else is required. This is the subject matter of Chapter 7.

## NOTES

1. The competitive equilibrium is determinate, given product and input prices, an initial resource endowment, and unattenuated property and exchange rights.
2. For a compact statement of the decision environment contemplated by neoclassical theory see Demsetz (1996, pp. 4–5).
3. See Wong (1973, p. 317), for the conditions which must be satisfied if an assumption is to be 'realistic'. The essential point is that, whereas 'economists...simply stopped worrying about the realism of micro-assumptions (after Friedman 1953)', as we shall see, economics cannot 'declare independence' from psychology [and other] sciences (Lewin 1996, p. 1319).
4. For representative critiques of economic man, see Cox and Epstein (1989), Elster (1989), Furubotn (1994), Knox (1999), Nelson (1995), North (1994), Sen (1995), Thaler (2000), Tversky and Thaler (1990).
5. Noting that 'The histories of economics and biology intertwine', Robson 'advocates consideration of the biological basis of economic behavior' (2001, p. 11). Indeed, recent experimental results involving equity, reciprocity and competition have been rationalized by appeal to evolutionary biology (Bolton and Ockenfels 2000).
6. Henrich (2000) presents evidence that 'economic decisions and economic reasoning may be heavily influenced by cultural differences – that is, by socially transmitted rules about how to behave in certain circumstances (economic or otherwise) that may vary from group to group as a consequence of different cultural evolutionary trajectories'. In view of this social learning, he concludes that 'the assumption that humans share the same economic decision-making processes must be reconsidered' (p. 973). For experimental evidence on the effect of group attachment and social learning on economic behavior see Harbough and Krause (2000). For a survey of game theoretic and empirical efforts which suggest that cooperative behavior may be attributed to the development of social norms, see Ostrom (2000). See also Fehr and Gächter (2000). For a characterization of a sociological view of the endogeneity of preference structures, see Baron and Hannan (1994, p. 1117). Finally, for a discussion of the empirical problems which attend the use of outcome data

to distinguish among endogeneity interactions, 'contextual interactions' and 'correlated effects', see Manski (2000, pp. 128–130).

7. Arguably, the possibility that learning may alter preference structures animated the Stigler and Becker effort (1977) to show that addiction, habit formation and other intertemporal phenomena are consistent with the stability of 'metapreferences'. Yet, these 'underlying preferences' defined over 'fundamental aspects of life' can only be inferred; they do not govern choices among purchasable economic goods (Aaron 1994, p. 6). The essential difficulty is that any observed behavior can be ascribed to 'underlying preferences'. It follows that models employing this approach are not disconfirmable (Pollak 1985, pp. 584–585). Indeed, in his 1993 Nobel lecture Gary Becker observed that 'Actions are constrained by income, time, imperfect memory and calculating capacities, and other limited resources'. Granting this, he concludes that 'My work may have sometimes assumed too much rationality' (Becker 1993, p. 402). For more on the Stigler and Becker approach see Furubotn (1994) and Roth (1998). For applications of 'habit formation' and 'habit stocks' to macroeconomic problems, see Fuhrer (2000) and Carroll, Overland and Weil (2000). For a discussion of the problems which attend the use of the 'representative consumer' construct in macroeconomic models, see Carroll (2000).
8. For a model which includes moral concerns in utility functions and constraints, see Dowell, Goldfarb and Griffith (1998).
9. Starmer (2000, p. 377) observes that 'Perhaps "anomalies" in choice behavior will turn out to be insignificant for a broad range of problems', but 'the data we have suggests that choice behavior displays complex patterns in even very simple contexts'. Given this, he asks 'is there a good reason for thinking that behavior in a more complex reality will better conform to our simple models?' His response to his rhetorical question is unambiguous: 'It would surely be genuinely surprising if that were true'. See also Conlisk (1996) and Luzzati (1999).
10. Rabin and Thaler (2001, p. 230) put the matter straightforwardly:

    For nearly 50 years, economists have been fending off researchers who have identified clear departures from expected utility....

    In terms of its mathematical elegance, tractability, and normative appeal, the expected utility model clearly has 'beautiful plumage'. But when the model is plainly wrong and frequently misleading, at some point economists must conclude that the plumage doesn't enter into it.

    Given this, they ask, 'What should expected utility theory be replaced with?'
11. Richard Thaler (2000) has made 'six bold predictions about how economics will develop over the next couple decades' (p. 134). *Inter alia*, he predicts that 'Homo Economicus Will Begin Losing IQ, Reversing a 50-year Trend' (p. 134), that 'Economists Will Study Human Cognition' (p. 137), and that 'Homo Economicus Will Become More Emotional' (p. 139). Reduced to its essentials, he predicts that 'Homo Economicus will evolve into Homo Sapiens' (p. 140). Finally, Foster (2000) observes that, whereas Conlisk (1996) 'depicts bounded rationality as mainly concerned with cognitive problems...accumulated evidence in psychology...suggests that economic rationality is bounded not only by cognitive limitations but also by emotional considerations' (p. 174).
12. See also Miller (1997, p. 1198); Buchanan (1994b, Chapter 3); Furubotn and Richter (1997, pp. 417–420); Prybyla (1995) and Krug (1999). While he focuses on development economics, Myerson (1999) indirectly makes a generic point of immediate relevance: 'In development economics, an exclusive methodological reliance on price theory can lead naturally to a focus on those aspects of the developing economy that can be formulated within the terms of price theory'. Granting this, he perceives 'a relative neglect of other fundamental problems such as crime and corruption, which can undermine the system of property rights that price theory assumes' (p. 1080).
13. Whereas sociologists regard preferences and values as 'results of enduring exchanges and social contracts' (Baron and Hannan 1994, p. 1117), economists characteristically employ

the convention adopted by Kenneth Arrow (1951, p. 7): 'we will...assume...that individual values are taken as data and are not capable of being altered by the decision process itself'.

14. The Nobel laureate econometrician Trygve Haavelmo agrees. He has suggested that economics generally, and econometrics in particular, must take account of the relationships between 'economic results' and the 'structure of rules and regulations within which the members of society have to operate' (1997, p. 15).
15. For more on Smith's notion of 'sympathy', see Muller (1993, Chapter 8).
16. Warke (2000) notes both that 'modern economic theory is essentially utilitarian with one significant exception: its abandonment of a multi-dimensional conception of utility', and that 'Non-utilitarian ethics, by contrast, attains determinate optima by means of an *a priori* designation of intrinsic worth' (p. 373). The second point is consistent with the theme which underlies this book: I take as given the Kantian prior commitment to the moral equivalence of persons (Chapter 1).
17. See also Buchanan (1994b, pp. 82–83).
18. See also Stigler (1987, pp. 136–138); Furubotn (1965); Roth (1974).
19. The essential point is that cognitive limitations both militate against optimizing solutions and account for the disparity between decision makers' objective and subjectively perceived decision environments. This phenomenon, referred to earlier as the competence–difficulty gap, has as one if its corollaries uncertainty about how to use information. Indeed, in the face of complexity, decision makers 'systematically restrict the use and acquisition of information compared to that potentially available' (Heiner 1983, p. 564). See also Wilde, LeBaron and Israelsen (1985, p. 407).
20. *Inter alia*, each producer must decide whether to choose among the subset of technical options about which something is known – the *a priori* technical array – or to choose among an expanded array which includes technical options about which information has been secured. The solution to these and related decision problems is conditioned by subjective prior stocks of knowledge, by potentially disparate desiderata, and by subjectively chosen decision methods. For an approach to the choice of technique problem see Roth (1997).
21. Whatever else is said, it is useful to recall that preference satisfaction may not be an adequate conception of individual and, *pari passu*, 'social' well-being (§ 2.2).
22. The same caveat applies, *mutatis mutandis*, to the 'compensation principle' (§ 5.3).
23. For more on the inadequacy of the fundamental welfare theorems as a theory of the state, see Brennan (1995, pp. 142–152).

# 7. The contractarian approach to government

## 7.1 THE PRIOR MORAL COMMITMENT: A REPRISE

As we have seen, the contractarian enterprise has developed along two conceptual loci. For reasons discussed in Section 1.4, it is the Kantian/Rawlsian variant which informs the balance of this book. *Inter alia*, this involves a prior commitment to the moral equivalence of persons (§ 1.2) and to the moral law or categorical imperative (CI) (§ 1.3). While the CI may be expressed in a number of ways, the Formula of the End in Itself demands that the autonomy, agency, independence, self-determination and dignity of morally equivalent persons be respected. On this account, it is not persons' 'utility' or 'happiness' that is morally exigent. Rather, the imperative is to accord all persons impartial consideration. It follows, *pari passu*, that whereas consequentialist social welfare theory regards the maximization of aggregative utility as the ultimate desideratum or 'public good', the CI is procedural or contractarian. The demand for equal consideration requires both that rights be given lexical priority, and that just – in the sense of impartial – institutions be promoted. Thus, whereas consequentialist social welfare theory can accommodate neither the moral force of rights (§ 2.1) nor an explicit theory of justice (§ 2.23), the Kantian/Rawlsian project regards rights as morally exigent, and defines justice as impartiality (§ 2.22).

## 7.2 THE INDETERMINACY OF 'ENDS'

Given its procedural orientation the Kantian/Rawlsian (hereafter contractarian) enterprise does not regard 'outcomes' as the subject of normative appraisal. If nothing else were said, the indeterminacy of consequentialist or outcomes-based social welfare theory (Chapter 6) suggests the efficacy of this approach.[1] Equally important, significant logical, empirical and ontological problems attend the notion of a supraindividual public good which, on consequentialist logic, ought to be promoted (§ 3.2). Finally, the fact that utilitarian considerations can always trump rights (§ 2.1) opens the door to all manner of casuistries.

*Inter alia*, utilitarian social welfare theory has been deployed to rationalize 'efficiency-enhancing' corruption (§ 5.1).

The decisive consideration is, however, that the autonomy, agency, independence, self-determination and dignity of morally equivalent persons possessed of free will and complex, endogenously determined preference and value structures (§ 6.2) generates an institutional rather than an outcomes-based imperative. Reduced to its essentials, individuals should be free to pursue their objectives – whatever they may be – subject to the constraints imposed by respect for rights and by just or impartial institutions.[2] Indeed, the imperative of impartial institutional design requires that 'final ends and desires' be ignored (Rawls [1989] 1999, p. 502).

## 7.3 PROCEDURAL JUSTICE AND THE INSTITUTIONAL IMPERATIVE

Central to the contractarian enterprise is the idea of a social contract which embodies a basic principle of impartial deliberation (§ 1.4). What is envisioned is an 'original position' characterized by a 'veil of ignorance' (§ 1.5). In effect, the choice among principles of justice – of institutional design – requires that individuals not act 'heteronomously'; that they not be influenced by persons' social position, natural endowments, life plans, preference structures or 'ends'. It is in this sense that the contractarian model of politics 'depends not at all on the postulated motivation of the individual actor' (Brennan and Buchanan 1985, p. 42). Rather, the moral equivalence of persons demands that the decision environment within which they pursue their individual goals – including, *pari passu*, their individuated, subjective perceptions of the 'public good' – contemplate respect for rights and impartial institutions (§ 3.2).

A likely response to the impartial deliberation construal is that it has no empirical counterpart; that 'people do not behave that way'. In fact, the original position/veil of ignorance construal is properly understood to be 'a schematic representation of a particular mental process of at least some, and perhaps most, human beings' (Dworkin 1978, p. 158). According to this, the original position 'may be viewed…as a procedural interpretation of Kant's conception of autonomy and the categorical imperative' (Rawls 1971, p. 256):[3]

> an essential feature of Kant's moral constructivism is that the first principles of right and justice are seen as specified by a procedure of construction (the CI procedure) the form and structure of which mirrors our free moral personality as both reasonable and rational. This conception of the person he regards as implicit in our every day moral consciousness…. This conception is found in how we

represent to ourselves our free and equal moral personality in every day life (Rawls [1989] 1999, p. 512).

The impartial deliberation construal does not, therefore, demand that persons – as 'legislators' in the 'kingdom of ends' (§ 1.3) – *actually* be deprived of knowledge of all persons' social positions, natural endowments, life plans or preference structures (§§ 1.4 and 1.5). Rather, the presumption is that, in their everyday lives, free and morally equivalent persons have a duty both to respect the rights of others and to promote just, in the sense of impartial, institutions. Given this imperative, the Kantian/Rawlsian contract device is a procedural heuristic:

> It can render our judgements more determinate (contractual agreements must be explicitly and publicly formulated), render them more vivid (the veil of ignorance is a vivid way of expressing the moral requirements of putting ourselves in other peoples' shoes), and can dramatize our commitment to them (the veil of ignorance dramatizes the claim that we would accept a certain principle however it affected us). In these and other ways, the contract device illuminates the basic ideas of morality as impartiality, even if it cannot help defend those ideas (Kymlicka 1993, p. 193).[4]

On this account agreement among persons with conflicting aims and interests relies upon the logic that 'whoever applies the CI procedure, roughly the same judgments are reached, provided the procedure is applied intelligently and conscientiously, and against the background of roughly the same beliefs and information' (Rawls [1989] 1999, p. 516). Granting this, the CI procedure – or moral law – 'is the only way for us to construct a unified public code of conduct without falling into heteronomy' (p. 521).[5]

Given that the CI procedure 'specifies a scope within which permissible ends must fall, as well as limits on means that can be adopted in the pursuit of these ends' (Rawls [1989] 1999, p. 524), we can adduce the implications for constitutional and conflictual or day-to-day politics (§ 1.7). Recall first that the moral equivalence of persons has an analog in political philosophy (§ 1.7). The principle of equal participation (Rawls 1971, pp. 221–222) implies an institutional imperative (p. 227). Reduced to its essentials, the principle contemplates a constitutional democracy (Rawls 1971, pp. 222, 243 and 275).[6] Whereas consequentialist social welfare theory can provide only a contingent justification of constitutional democracy (§ 3.3), the moral equivalence of persons – and, *pari passu*, the principle of equal participation – demands that the constitution give lexical priority to rights, and that the constitutional rules of the conflictual politics game be consonant with the emergence of just, in the sense of impartial, laws (Rawls 1971, pp. 221 and 227).

## 7.4 THE GENERALITY PRINCIPLE

While the internal and external morality of the law will be taken up below (§ 8.2), it is sufficient for present purposes to note that equality under the idealized rule of law is consistent with the contractarian notion of justice as impartiality. Indeed, insofar as the law contemplates the greatest possible equal liberty (Rawls 1971, pp. 239–240), it meets the first test of contractarian justice; namely, the lexical priority of rights.[7]

The essential idea is that, from the contractarian perspective, 'Law... becomes legitimate only if all persons could have agreed conceptually, and such agreement is most likely when all persons affected are generally and reciprocally constrained in their behavior' (Buchanan and Congleton 1998, p. 8). The logic is that, *inter alia*, rights protection and the 'stability of social cooperation' (Rawls 1971, p. 240) require agreement on constraints on behavior (p. 235), and these constraints will, presumably, be mutually beneficial to all parties. Yet, whatever else is said, absent generality or impartiality under and by it, the law cannot be regarded as just. It cannot, in short, be consistent with the moral equivalence of persons.

If the idealized rule of law embodies a generality or impartiality principle, the same cannot be said of conflictual or day-to-day politics. Perhaps because of the continuing dominance of the social welfare theory paradigm, 'romanticized politics remains monolithic; the "good" is defined uniquely by the collective agency of the state' (Buchanan and Congleton 1998, p. XI).[8] In effect, the 'benevolent despot' is presumed to act in the supraindividual interest of the majority.[9] Yet, as Buchanan and Congleton have emphasized, 'As it operates, [because] postconstitutional politics is majoritarian, [it is], naturally, discriminatory to the extent that participants promote separable interests' (1998, p. 12).[10] In contractarian logic, therefore, postconstitutional or conflictual day-to-day politics is neither moral nor, *pari passu*, legitimate:

> discriminatory politics cannot pass the contractarian test. In reflective equilibrium and behind a veil of ignorance/uncertainty, persons could never agree to the establishment of political institutions that are predicted to discriminate explicitly in their operation. The politics of discrimination would not meet the agreement criterion that defines fairness or justice. And, also importantly, such a politics would necessarily be inefficient in a resource-wasting sense (Buchananan and Congleton 1998, p. 11).

The allusion to the 'inefficiency' of discriminatory conflictual politics is predicated on the idea that it provides incentive for resource-wasting rent seeking activity (§ 5.3).[11] While more will be said about this (§ 8.1), the essential idea is that discriminatory conflictual politics is both unjust and *politically* inefficient.

'Cycling' is a characteristic feature of majoritarian democracy (Arrow 1951; Black 1958). In effect, majority coalitions may extract in-period benefits from, and/or impose costs upon, members of the extant minority. Yet this in-period discrimination may be accepted on the 'implicit understanding [that] dominant coalitions rotate sequentially over electoral periods' (Buchanan and Congleton 1998, pp. 19–20). Whatever else is said, the 'cycling' of discriminatory treatment may properly be characterized as the 'politics of taking' (p. 19).

While the politics of taking is both unjust and wasteful, majoritarian agreement does not contemplate any 'protected sphere of activity' (p. 19). Yet, if the subject matter of this, quite literally, conflictual politics cannot be limited *a priori*, it is proper to ask whether procedural limits can be imposed.

It is useful first to acknowledge that the 'external morality of the law consists in the substantive aims or values that particular legal rules seek to promote' (Ten 1995, p. 397). From the contractarian perspective the substantive aims of the idealized rule of law consist in rights protection and the impartial consideration of the interests of all. Given this Kantian/Rawlsian perspective it is appropriate that the generality or impartiality constraint be extended to conflictual politics (Buchanan and Congleton 1998, p. 7).

We proceed on the presumption, already noted, that conflictual politics is majoritarian and, *pari passu*, discriminatory. Granting this, a generality or impartiality constraint must be embedded in the *rules* of the conflictual politics game. What is required, in short, is constitutional change. The crucial point is that

> At the constitutional level, *identifiable* self-interest is not present in terms of external characteristics. The self-interest of the individual participant at this level leads him to take a position as a 'representative' or 'randomly distributed' participant in the succession of collective choices anticipated. Therefore, he may tend to act from self-interest, *as if* he were choosing the best set of rules for the social group (Buchanan and Tullock 1962, p. 96).

In effect, veil of ignorance-situated agreement on a generality or impartiality constraint, while not possible at the postconstitutional or conflictual stage, is possible at the constitutional level. While more will be said about this below (§ 8.3), the essential idea is that, if majoritarian cycling is recognized, 'it may become rational for the members of the ruling majority coalition to support the constitutional change that will incorporate the generality principle, even in the understanding that adoption of such a rule will mean foregoing current period gains from discriminatory exploitation' (Buchanan and Congleton 1998, p. 57).

It seems clear, then, that a generality or impartiality constraint can emerge at the constitutional stage. The constitutional imperative to treat each person symmetrically is both consistent with the moral equivalence of persons (§ 1.2) and *politically* efficient. Equally important, impartial treatment of persons at the postconstitutional stage provides a *raison d'être* for majoritarian democracy. Rather than facilitating the cyclical extraction of value by one coalition from another, generality-constrained majoritarian democracy may be regarded as the *deus ex machina* for impartial deliberation.[12] Properly construed, like the law, the legitimacy of in-period conflictual politics depends upon agreement.[13] Yet, as Buchanan and Congleton have argued, 'agreement is most likely when all persons affected are generally and reciprocally constrained in their behavior' (1998, p. 8). A constitutionally imposed generality or impartiality rule provides such a constraint.[14]

Finally, given the indeterminacy of both the efficiency frontier and the social welfare function (Chapter 6), a constitutionally mandated generality constraint would militate against *ad hoc* deployment of the first and second fundamental welfare theorems (§§ 6.5 and 6.6). *Inter alia*, government market and redistributional interventions would not be animated on the presumption that the government – the 'benevolent despot' – 'can do better' (§ 5.2). Instead, government policy would find its normative basis in individual perceptions of the public good – subject to the constraint that rights are respected, and all persons are impartially treated.

## NOTES

1. Agnosticism with respect to individuals' malleable and adaptive goals or 'ends' is consistent with the Hayekian view that 'The peculiar character of the problem of a rational economic order is determined precisely by the fact that the knowledge of the circumstances of which we must make use never exists in concentrated form but solely as the dispersed bits of incomplete and frequently contradictory knowledge which all the separate individuals possess' (Hayek 1948, p. 77). Moreover, as Manski has observed, 'empirical analysis of social interactions has lagged far behind theory, with distressing consequences' (2000, p. 123). *Inter alia*, the analysis is complicated by the 'reflection problem' (pp. 128–130).
2. 'Ends' are 'permissible' only insofar as they respect the limits of the CI, the moral law (Rawls [1989] 1999, pp. 507, 509 and 524). Moreover, the CI procedure places 'limits on the means that can be adopted in the pursuit of these ends' (p. 524). Finally, 'the constraints on the CI-procedure are valid for all reasonable and rational persons, no matter what their natural desires and inclinations' (p. 524).
3. For more on Kant's notion of 'autonomy', see § 1.2.
4. See also Hampton (1995, p. 387).
5. Again, 'heteronomy' connotes the idea that, when account is taken of persons' social positions, natural endowments and other, contingent phenomena, judgements and decisions cannot be impartial. See § 1.5, Kant ([1785] 1988, pp. 70–71) and Rawls (1971, p. 252).
6. See also Rawls ([1989] 1999, p. 526), Hampton (1995, pp. 390–392), and O'Neill (1993, p. 180).
7. It should be noted, however, that 'a regime of equal liberties among all persons may or

may not be a regime of extensive liberties' (Buchanan and Congleton 1998, p. 8). See also Rawls (1971, pp. 243–251).

8. See, especially, §§ 3.2, 3.3, 4.4, 5.2 and 5.3.
9. For an adumbration and critique of the 'omniscient, omnipotent, benevolent' government see Dixit (1996). See also §§ 4.4, 5.2 and 5.3.
10. In his discussion of 'Political Justice and the Constitution', John Rawls assumes 'that the main variation in the extent of equal political liberty lies in the degree to which the constitution is majoritarian' (1971, p. 224).
11. See also Buchanan and Congleton (1998, p. 40).
12. There is a literature which suggests that the 'propensity to cooperate' may be based, in part, on the development and growth of informal institutions or social norms (Ostrom 2000). Perhaps the formal institutionalization of a generality or impartiality constraint may also enhance the 'propensity to cooperate'. See also Rawls (1971, pp. 233–234).
13. It should be obvious that the 'legitimacy' of government institutions is important to a society. Schneider and Enste (2000, p. 107) have argued, for example, that

    > The analysis of causes shows that an increasing burden of taxation and social security payments, combined with rising state regulatory activities and labor market restrictions (e.g., forced reduction in working hours), are the major driving forces for the size and growth of the shadow economy. But an interdisciplinary approach seems to be necessary for a more comprehensive analysis, which would consider aspects like tax morale, perceived fairness of the tax system, and constitutional aspects as well.

14. For more on the CI procedure as a side-constraint on action see O'Neill (1993, p. 182).

# 8. The rules of the political game

## 8.1 ECONOMIC VS. POLITICAL EFFICIENCY

The efficiency concept which has been repeatedly invoked, Pareto optimality, is distinguished from productive efficiency, the 'output maximizing' property imputed to the neoclassical flow–flow production function (§ 4.2). Both of these efficiency construals may be distinguished from 'political' efficiency. The latter is understood to 'describe the efficacy of differing institutions in reducing or eliminating the incentives for participants to invest resources in rent seeking aimed to secure discriminatory advantage through majoritarian exploitation' (Buchanan and Congleton 1998, p. 40). The balance of this book is informed by the notion that the 'basic principle of collective political order, that of equal treatment' (Buchanan [1975] 2000, p. 51) is both consistent with the moral equivalence of persons (§ 1.2) and *politically* efficient (§ 7.4). The presumption is, then, that a constitutionally embedded generality or impartiality constraint militates against the resource-wasting rent seeking activity which characterizes conflictual or postconstitutional politics.

While some might argue that political efficiency may be gained at the expense of Paretian optimality or efficiency, the logic of Chapter 6 suggests that the latter is, in fact, an indeterminate standard. Yet, even if it were supposed that first-best Paretian optimality can meaningfully be deployed as a standard of normative appraisal, we have seen that there can be no presumption that, in the presence of 'market failure', the 'government can do better' (§ 5.2). Moreover, as has been repeatedly emphasized, the logic of social welfare theory can be deployed to rationalize 'efficiency-enhancing' corruption by, *inter alia*, government officials (§ 5.1). Finally, because it is utilitarian, consequentialist social welfare theory cannot accommodate the moral force of rights (§ 2.1). It follows, *mutatis mutandis*, that the path to the Paretian welfare surface – the efficiency frontier – is compromised (§ 6.4).

Even if these objections were set aside, the suitability of Paretian efficiency as a standard of normative appraisal is compromised by its inability to accommodate an explicit understanding of justice (§ 2.2).[1]

Finally, even if one were to suppose that the efficiency frontier is determinate, the discriminatory 'cycling' which is characteristic of majoritarian democracy (§ 7.4) militates against the achievement of 'first-best Paretian optima'. Granting this,

> The gains in political efficiency that the [generality] constraint ensures would seem to more than offset any possible loss in ideal or potential allocative efficiency, defined in the usual way – an efficiency that could scarcely be realized under any recognizable political regime and certainly not one that gives scope for the workings of majoritarian institutions (Buchanan and Congleton 1998, p. 41).

These considerations suggest that the moral imperative is not, as consequentialist social welfare theory suggests, to promote Pareto optimal outcomes. Stated differently – and roughly – the objective should not be to 'get the prices right'. Rather, the imperative should be to 'get the institutions right'. Given the moral equivalence of persons (§ 7.1) this reduces to the duty both to accord rights lexical priority and to promote just, in the sense of impartial, institutions. What is required, in short, is the greatest possible liberty under the law, and nondiscriminatory treatment under a postconstitutional political regime (§ 7.3).[2]

## 8.2 THE GENERALITY PRINCIPLE AND THE RULE OF LAW

My point of departure is John Rawls's observation that

> the connection of the rule of law with liberty is clear enough. Liberty...is a complex of rights and duties, defined by institutions.... The principle of legality has a firm foundation...in the agreement of rational persons to establish for themselves the greatest equal liberty. To be confident in the possession and exercise of these freedoms, the citizens of a well-ordered society will normally want the rule of law maintained (1971, pp. 239–240).

Recall first that the principle of equal liberty – or of equal participation when applied to the political procedure defined by the constitution (Rawls 1971, p. 221) – finds its normative basis in the moral equivalence of persons (§ 1.2). The categorical imperative, in turn, demands that we respect the autonomy, agency, independence, self-determination and dignity of morally equivalent persons (§ 1.3). The external morality, or the substantive aims or values that, on contractarian terms, the law ought to promote finds expression in these ideas (Ten 1995, p. 397). According to this, 'the conception of formal justice, the regular and impartial administration of public rules, becomes the rule of law when applied to the legal system' (Rawls 1971, p. 235).

The external morality of the law demands, then, that the greatest possible equal liberty be promoted. This is true both at the constitutional (Rawls 1971, pp. 221–228) and at the postconstitutional stage.[3] At the constitutional level, the principle of equal liberty (or equal participation when applied to political procedures) means that each vote has approximately the same weight, that members of the legislature – with one vote each – represent the same number of electors, and that all citizens have equal access to public office (p. 223). The *extent* of equal liberty or of equal participation is defined as 'the degree to which the procedure of (bare) majority rule is restricted by the mechanisms of constitutionalism' (p. 228). Rawls states that majorities have 'final authority' on 'devices which serve to limit the scope of majority rule', subject to the constraint that 'limits on the extent of the principle of [equal] participation [must] fall equally upon everyone' (p. 228). For its part, the justification for such limits is that they 'protect the other freedoms' (p. 229). For example, 'A bill of rights may remove certain liberties from majority regulation altogether, and the separation of powers with judicial review may slow down the pace of legislative change' (p. 228). Finally, and of particular importance to postconstitutional or conflictual politics, the *worth* or value of equal political participation requires that the constitution 'underwrite a fair opportunity to take part in and to influence the political process' (p. 224). *Inter alia*, this requires that the constitution protect freedom of speech, assembly, thought and conscience. Moreover, all citizens 'should have the means to be informed about political issues' (p. 225). The imperative, in short, is to prevent the pleadings of the 'more advantaged social and economic interests' from receiving 'excessive attention' (p. 226).[4]

In sum, the principle of equal liberty (or equal participation when applied to political procedures) demands that a constitution sets up 'a form of fair rivalry for political office and authority' in which, *inter alia*, 'those in authority' – the elected representatives – 'must seek first to pass just and effective legislation…and secondly, they must further their constituents' other interests insofar as they are consistent with justice' (Rawls 1971, p. 227).[5] These considerations inform the discussion in Chapter 9.

While the external morality of the law finds its basis in the moral equivalence of persons, its internal morality is summarized by 'the precepts of justice associated with the rule of law'. These precepts, in turn, 'are those that would be followed by any system of rules which perfectly embodied the idea of a legal system' (Rawls 1971, p. 236).

According to Lon Fuller (1971) there are eight such precepts or principles : (1) The law should be general in the sense that it lays down general standards of conduct; (2) Laws should be promulgated or made known to those to whom they apply; (3) Laws should be prospective rather than retroactive; (4) Laws should be clear; (5) Laws should not be contradictory; (6) Laws should not demand the impossible; (7) Laws should not be changed frequently; and (8) Laws should require a congruence between official action and the relevant statutes.

Fuller's adumbration of the principles of internal morality of the law is roughly congruent with Rawls's account of the 'precepts of justice associated with the rule of law' (1971, pp. 236–239). We need add only that 'there are those precepts defining the notion of natural justice. These are guidelines intended to preserve the integrity of the judicial process'. *Inter alia*, 'A conscientious effort must be made to determine whether an infraction has taken place and to impose the correct penalty' (pp. 238–239).

The upshot is that the principle of equal liberty, or equal participation when applied to the political procedure defined by the constitution, finds its normative basis in the moral equivalence of persons. It follows that the external morality of the law, both at the constitutional and at the post-constitutional or conflictual politics stage, demands that the greatest possible equal liberty be promoted, that each person has a fair opportunity to take part in and to influence the political process, and that elected representatives pass just, in the sense of impartial, legislation. For its part, the internal morality of the law demands that laws be general, be made known, be prospective, and be clear and not contradictory. Moreover, laws must not demand the impossible, they must not be changed frequently, and they should require that official action be congruent with the law. These ideas, like those associated with the external morality of the law, inform the discussion in Chapter 9.

## 8.3 INSTITUTIONALIZED IMPARTIALITY

Reduced to its essentials, the argument developed above is that the 'basic principle of collective political order, that of equal treatment' (Buchanan [1975] 2000, p. 51) is both consistent with the moral equivalence of persons and politically efficient. Granting this, justice – in the sense of impartiality – demands that the generality principle be incorporated both in the rule of law, and in the constitutional rules of the conflictual politics game:

> The effective operation of democratic government, in its fiscal as well as its nonfiscal aspects, requires the adherence of its citizens to what may be called the 'constitutional attitude'....government can function properly only if a large proportion of its day-to-day operations take place within a quasi-permanent constitutional structure. Individuals, and groups, must recognize the importance of constitutional-institutional continuity, and the dependence of democratic process on firm adherence to such continuity. If this is not recognized, and if individuals come to consider governmental processes as nothing more than available means through which separate coalitions can exploit each other, democracy cannot, and should not, survive (Buchanan [1967] 1999, pp. 301–302).

While appeal to a generality constraint on the operation of majority rule politics finds its normative foundation in a prior commitment to the moral equivalence of persons, the logic of discriminatory majoritarian cycling (§ 7.4) underscores the practical necessity of such a procedural rule. Nothing less than the legitimacy of majoritarian democracy is at stake. If trust is instrumentally important to the functioning of increasingly impersonal markets, it is no less important to the functioning of political markets.

Given that a constitutionally embedded generality constraint is both morally exigent and instrumentally important, a question, tentatively answered in § 7.4, remains: Can the requisite constitutional change be achieved?

The 'publicness' of constitutional provisions and of the rule of law must, of course, be acknowledged. In effect, 'the structure of law...represents social or public capital stock, the yield from which accrues through a sequence of time periods' (Buchanan [1975] 2000, p. 156). Given the publicness and (potential) durability of a constitutional change two problems must be faced. On the one hand, the present value of the net expected benefits to an idealized person who expects to live forever will exceed that of the participatory agent whose planning horizon is finite (pp. 157–158). On the other hand, when the expected benefits of constitutional rule changes accrue publicly, one might plausibly ask, 'Who are to take upon themselves the personal burden of designing provisional proposals for basic changes in the rules?' (Brennan and Buchanan [1985] 2000, p. 160). In short, the lack of congruence between ideal and actual planning horizons may, when coupled with the 'free rider' problem, militate against constitutional change.

Given the moral exigency, instrumental importance and publicness of the generality principle it seems clear that constitutional dialogue must be encouraged (Buchanan [1989] 1999, p. 369). The dialogue may be facilitated by what James Buchanan has called 'preaching'.[6] According to Buchanan, the individual, as a citizen, must be made to understand that he has an 'ethical responsibility of full and informed participation in a continuing constitutional convention' (p. 372). Failure to attend to this responsibility has resulted in the emergence of a postconstitutional or conflictual politics 'that is almost exclusively dominated by and derivative from the strategic choices made by competing interests in disregard of the effects on political structure' (p. 372).

Presumptively, the notion that the moral equivalence of persons demands that they be treated impartially can be fashioned into 'models amenable to public comprehension' (Buchanan [1975] 2000, p. 227). So, too, can the idea that discriminatory conflictual politics are both incompatible with the moral equivalence of persons, and reflective of the rent seeking which is corrosive of trust and the legitimacy of government. Yet, if these ideas are judged to be 'too abstract', the individual, as citizen, should be made to understand that, given majoritarian cycling, a generality constraint is in his self-interest (§ 7.4). In effect, the individual has incentive to agree to a constitutionally embedded generality constraint because he cannot 'see the future'. If he is not myopic he will understand that his membership in the extant dominant majority does not ensure that he will not, in the future, be a member of an exploited minority. Granting this,

> The self-interest of the individual participant at [the constitutional] level leads him to take a position as a 'representative' or 'randomly distributed' participant in the succession of collective choices anticipated. Therefore, he may tend to act, from self-interest, *as if* he were choosing the best set of rules of the social group (Buchanan and Tullock 1962, p. 96).

In sum, while it is self-interest that animates her thinking, it is ignorance of her future state that accounts for what is, in effect, the incentive to agree on a veil of ignorance-situated agreement on a generality or impartiality constraint.

Granting the logic of what has been said, I proceed on the assumption that a generality constraint *can* emerge at the constitutional level. With this in mind, I turn to a discussion of the impact of such a constraint on day-to-day conflictual politics.

## NOTES

1. The 'time-slice' principle of justice implicit in the theory is, to paraphrase Nozick, inadequate (§ 2.24). It is appropriate again to emphasize that these and other considerations suggest that deployments of the second fundamental welfare theorem must be regarded as *ad hoc* (§ 5.3).
2. Buchanan and Congleton argue that the generality or impartiality standard is met 'when political actions apply to all persons independently of membership in a dominant coalition or an effective interest group' (1998, p. XI).
3. Ronald Dworkin bases his theory of legislative rights on 'John Rawls's powerful and influential theory of justice, that our intuitions about justice presume not only that people have rights but that one right among them is fundamental and axiomatic. This...is a distinct conception of the right to equality, which I call the right to equal concern and respect' (1978, p. XII). See also pp. 180–183.
4. It is interesting that the 'father of modern economics' (Tribe 1999, p. 609) produced a book which may be regarded as an adumbration of attempts by individuals and groups to promote their own interests. See, for example, Adam Smith ([1776], 1976, pp. 452–472). We should note also that, in his development of a general theory of rights – a theory based on equality – Ronald Dworkin assumes the acceptance of certain 'postulates of political morality'. Among these is the postulate that '[Government] must not distribute goods or opportunities unequally on the ground that some citizens are entitled to more because they are worthy of more concern' (1978, pp. 272–273).
5. It is worth emphasizing that 'just' legislation is understood to be impartial legislation.
6. See, for example, Buchanan (1991, p. 186, 1994b, p. 80 and 1994a).

# 9. Playing by the generality rule

## 9.1 SOME PRELIMINARIES

This chapter deploys the Kantian/Rawlsian contractarian idea of the moral equivalence of persons in the normative appraisal of conflictual or day-to-day politics. The enterprise is informed, without further justificatory argument, by the following ideas: First, the moral equivalence of persons implies an institutional imperative. The essential ideas are that the agency, independence, self-determination and dignity of the individual demands that rights be accorded lexical priority, and that just in the sense of impartial institutions be promoted. *Inter alia*, this means that persons must be accorded the greatest possible equal liberty under and by constitutional and statutory law, and that the constitution – the rules of the game of post-constitutional or conflictual politics – embody a generality or impartiality constraint. Second, the argument takes as given that democratic politics is associated with majority rule, and that majoritarian cycling and resource-wasting rent seeking are defining characteristics of observable reality. Third, given the indeterminacy of the efficiency frontier and the logical, empirical and ontological problems associated with the social welfare function I reject *a priori* any rationale for 'government intervention' motivated by the first and second fundamental welfare theorems.

While the analysis is animated, in part, by the Buchanan–Congleton (1998) emphasis on political efficiency, there are substantive differences. First, whereas Buchanan and Congleton emphasize that the political efficiency gains associated with a constitutionally-embedded generality constraint would likely exceed any allocative efficiency losses, I regard the Paretian efficiency standard as indeterminate. Granting this, political efficiency gains are not properly characterized as 'net' gains or losses. Second, while Buchanan and Congleton acknowledge that 'The generality norm finds its post-Enlightenment philosophical foundation in Kant's normative precept for a personalized ethics and its institutional embodiment in the idealized rule of law that does, indeed, set out widely agreed upon criteria for the evaluation of legal structures' (1998, p. XI), the moral equivalence of persons does not *explicitly* animate their analysis (1998, p. 140). While the political efficiency of a constitutional generality constraint is acknowledged, the analysis deployed here is more heavily reliant on the imperative to treat morally equivalent persons impartially.

Finally, while the institutional imperatives which flow from the moral equivalence of persons have no spatio-temporal reference, I shall, for ease of exposition, occasionally appeal to the recent experience of the United States.

## 9.2 GENERALITY AND TAXATION

Let us first stipulate that the functioning of majoritarian democracy 'guarantees the emergence of discrimination in treatment between those who are members of the majority coalition and those who are not members' (Buchanan and Congleton 1998, p. 89). In the case of taxation, 'Adjusted for relative group size, members of the exploiting majority have more to gain from tax discrimination against the rich than against middle or low-income groups' (p. 91).

If tax rate 'progressivity' is a predictable outcome of majoritarian exploitation, the proliferation of 'preferential provisions' in tax codes such as special exclusions, exemptions, deductions, credits, deferrals, and differential tax rates applied to disparate 'tax bases' may be attributed to the rent seeking activity of 'special interest groups'.[1] Indeed, according to one account, 'the tax system is the single greatest source of lobbying activity in Washington' (Armey).

While much can be said about this, it is clear that a progressive tax rate structure violates the generality or impartiality standard. Stated differently, insofar as the tax code is a part of the body of statutory or post-constitutional law, tax rate discrimination is inconsistent with the external morality of the law (§ 8.2). *Inter alia*, the external morality of the law demands that 'those in authority...must seek first to pass just...legislation' (Rawls 1971, p. 227). For its part, the proliferation of complex tax code provisions – some of which are surreptitiously legislated – is inconsistent with the internal morality of the law (§ 8.2).

In Buchanan and Congleton's account, the 'ultimate purpose [of the generality norm] is to constrain majoritarian politics in order to prevent the natural tendency to use the taxing authority discriminatorily' (1998, p. 93). While I agree that political efficiency – the minimization of rent seeking – is an appropriate desideratum, the central issue is the discriminatory treatment of morally equivalent persons. Granting this, the institutional imperative is agreement on a constitutional generality or impartiality constraint. While Rawls has argued that 'since the burden of taxation is to be justly shared...a proportional expenditure tax may be part of the best tax scheme' (1971, p. 278), a uniform or flat tax defined on *all* income and contemplating *no* exemptions or deductions would also satisfy the impartiality standard.

## 9.3 GENERALITY AND GOVERNMENT OUTLAYS

It is generally understood that governments are engaged in the production, distribution and financing of pure public and potentially partitionable and excludable goods and services. What is perhaps less well known is that governments also engage in credit and insurance activities. While discussion of government insurance activities is addressed in § 9.6, it is important to recognize that, in the United States, 'The roles of Federal credit and insurance programs can be broadly classified into two: helping disadvantaged groups and correcting market failures. Subsidized Federal credit programs redistribute resources from the general taxpayer to disadvantaged regions or segments of the population' (Office of Management and Budget, *Analytical Perspectives*, 2001, p. 139).

Because government provision of pure public goods, of potentially partitionable and excludable goods, and of credit programs implicates different conceptual issues we shall consider them in order in the following subsections.

### 9.31 Pure Public Goods

The public goods discussion subsumed by § 5.2 will not be replicated here. It is sufficient to recall that the Pigovian efficiency standard is typically deployed to argue for public provision of such goods, and that a first-best Pareto optimal outcome requires that they be financed by taxes that are levied on the 'marginal benefit principle'. It follows that, when tastes are not homogeneous, optimal government provision of pure public goods contemplates tax-price discrimination. This, in turn, violates the generality criterion.

The difficulty here is clear. If the generality principle is interpreted to mean that public good demanders shall pay equal cost shares, the Pigovian efficiency standard will have been violated. That said, it is also clear that both technical and political considerations militate against deployment of the marginal benefit principle (§ 5.2). Granting this, 'Less than ideal general taxes on a broad objective tax base may yield better results than politicized benefit taxes' (Buchanan and Congleton 1998, p. 114). In their account, a uniform tax rate defined on a broad tax base can increase political stability: 'In such cases, everyone shares in the cost of providing the service and all would judge the service on the basis of costs and benefits received' (p. 115).

The essential idea is that there is no assurance that government provision of pure public goods and services can, in Pigovian logic, 'solve' the externality problem. There is, in short, no *a priori* reason to suppose that government 'ought' to supply such goods (§ 5.2). That said, when they *are* produced and financed by government, both the logic of majoritarian rent seeking and the moral equivalence of persons suggest a constitutional imperative. While generality does not determine the optimal tax base, the proceeds of a uniform tax rate imposed on that base should be earmarked for the provision of pure public goods and services.

## 9.32 Excludable Goods

If rent seeking is observable in the case of pure public goods, it is also characteristic of the market for excludable goods.

It is appropriate first to acknowledge that, in the United States, 60.7 per cent of federal government outlays fall under the rubric of a budget category styled 'Payments for Individuals' (Office of Management and Budget, *Historical Tables*, 2001, p. 115).[2] Another 17.2 per cent of total outlays consist in 'Net Interest' and 'All Other Grants'. The residual falls under the rubrics of 'National Defense' (16.1 per cent), 'All Other' (8.6 per cent), and 'Undistributed Offsetting Receipts' (–2.6 per cent) (p. 115).

Clearly, a significant portion of federal government outlays – roughly 78 per cent – does not contemplate government production of excludable goods. That said, the remaining outlay categories – 'National Defense' and 'All Other' – subsume what might be characterized as government intermediate demand. For example, in the case of 'National Defense', the services provided by government-procured capital goods – submarines, aircraft, tanks – constitute inputs in the 'national security production function'. For its part, the 'All Other' budget category incorporates such disparate activities or 'production functions' as international affairs, the administration of justice and agriculture.

The output of the national defense production function, national security, may be regarded as a pure public good. The same might be said of the international affairs and administration of justice production functions. For its part, the agriculture production function – and others like it – contemplate government's assumed role in the production of excludable, agricultural products. This role, as we shall see, is complex – and inconsistent with the generality principle.

Consider first the government's intermediate demand; its demand for inputs in its various production functions. As Buchanan and Congleton have emphasized,

> Application of the generality principle to the production of public goods and services requires that production decisions, themselves, should not confer benefits or costs on specific individuals, industries, or regions of the country. That is to say, the production, itself, of government services should not materially alter the distribution of wealth. Thus, complete generality requires the absence of significant relative price effects in the production of government services (1998, p. 110).

While it is acknowledged that size of market, locational economies, transaction-specific investment and productive factor immobility may militate against geographic dispersion of government input demand, it should also be recognized that these considerations are catalysts to supplier rent seeking. It follows that both political efficiency and the moral equivalence of persons demand that departures from the generality norm be *publicly* justified. *Inter alia*, this suggests that appropriations acts and contract authority be codified in statutes which satisfy the strictures of the internal morality of law (§ 8.2). Granting this, the moral equivalence of persons, the imperative to pass just laws, and the internal morality of law require that the constitution prohibit 'omnibus' laws; statutes which 'bundle' disparate spending programs (and revenue provisions) into a single, comprehensive act. Given their comprehensive nature such laws are, for the 'representative' citizen and, it might be argued, for the 'representative' Member of the legislative body, neither transparent nor comprehensible (§ 9.8).

If the government's demand for productive services must be constitutionally constrained, the same is true of its indirect involvement in the production of excludable goods. In the United States, for example,

> Through the Department of Agriculture (USDA), the Federal Government seeks to enhance the quality of life for the American people by supporting agricultural programs; ensuring a safe, affordable, nutritious and accessible food supply; conserving agricultural, forest, and range lands; supporting sound development of rural communities; providing economic opportunities for farm and rural residents; expanding global markets for agricultural and forest products and services; and working to reduce hunger in America and throughout the world (Office of Management and Budget, *Budget*, 2001, p. 53).

Given this adumbration of 'missions', during Fiscal Year 2000 federal government 'mandatory [agricultural] outlays' totalled about 32 billion dollars, direct loan disbursements exceeded 11 billion dollars, and guaranteed loans totalled more than 5.4 billion dollars (Table 7.1, p. 53).

While government credit activity is the subject matter of § 9.33, immediate interest centers on the 'mandatory outlays' contemplated by extant enabling legislation. It is significant that, while the 'missions' of the U.S. Department of Agriculture are broad in scope, the federal government identifies 'two big economic goals: (1) provide an economic safety net for farmers and ranchers; and (2) open, expand, and maintain global market opportunities for agricultural producers' (*Budget*, p. 53).

Consider first the 'economic safety net' goal. Under existing United States law the 'economic safety net' takes the form of income-support payments. During fiscal year 2000 such payments totalled 10 billion dollars (*Budget*, p. 55).[3]

If it is clear that such discriminatory payments encourage rent seeking activity, it is also clear that they violate the generality principle. While more will be said about transfer programs below (§ 9.5), both political efficiency and the moral equivalence of persons demand that discriminatory transfer programs be constitutionally prohibited. When, at the constitutional stage, agreement emerges that a transfer or redistribution scheme should be institutionalized (Buchanan [1967] 1999, p. 298), impartiality suggests that it take a particular form. In the event, 'A flat tax on all income combined with a set of equal-per-head demogrants would perhaps come closest to meeting the generality criterion while implementing redistribution through the fiscal process' (Buchanan and Congleton 1998, p. 118). What is, in any case, clear is that such a constitutionally constrained system would both minimize rent seeking and treat morally equivalent persons impartially.

The second, clearly articulated goal of United States' agricultural policy is to 'open, expand, and maintain global market opportunities for agricultural producers'. Given this 'key economic goal', the United States Department of Agriculture 'is authorized to spend more than 1 billion dollars in 2002 on a wide range of trade promotion programs that expand overseas market opportunities and develop long-term trade relationships with foreign countries' (Office of Management and Budget, *Budget* 2001, pp. 55–56). *Inter alia*, trade promotion activities include 'subsidies to export firms', and 'credit guarantees for the commercial financing of U.S. agricultural exports' (p. 56).

While government intervention in international markets is the subject matter of § 9.72, this much can be said: Whatever its intent, including *inter alia*, assisting exporters who confront 'unfairly subsidized overseas competitors' (p. 56), discriminatory 'trade promotion' activities violate the generality principle.[4] Either such activities should be constitutionally prohibited, or impartiality requires that *all* producers, whether or not they engage in international trade, should, under the Constitution, be accorded *equal* treatment. If this institutional imperative finds its basis in the moral equivalence of persons, the workings of majoritarian democracy suggest its political efficacy. Whatever else is said, resource-wasting rent seeking is characteristic of what has come to be characterized as 'trade policy'. In effect, a constitutional generality constraint would both respect the moral equivalence of persons and discourage rent seeking activity.

### 9.33 Generality and Government Credit Programs

Recall first that we consider credit programs under the rubric of 'Generality and Government Outlays' because, in the United States, 'Federal credit programs redistribute resources from the general taxpayer',[5] and because such programs implicate the production of excludable goods. In particular,

> Federal credit programs offer direct loans and loan guarantees for a wide range of activities, primarily housing, education, business and rural development, and exports. At the end of 2000, there were $241 billion in Federal direct loans outstanding and $1,043 billion in loan guarantees.
>
> The Federal Government also enhances credit availability for targeted sectors indirectly through Government-sponsored enterprises (GSEs) (Office of Management and Budget, *Analytical Perspectives*, 2001 p. 139).[6]

While the United States government employs 'market imperfection' or Paretian inefficiency arguments to 'justify' federal involvement in the housing, education, business and rural development and export markets (pp. 139–144), this is not the focus of my analysis. As we have seen (Chapter 5), the presence of 'market imperfections' does not imply that the government can do better. Moreover, because the efficiency frontier is indeterminate, Paretian efficiency is not a suitable device for normative public policy appraisal (Chapter 6).

Granting this, the focus here is upon the fundamentally discriminatory nature of government credit programs. The political inefficiency of such programs is itself a cause for concern. Plainly stated, the existence of these programs is a catalyst to resource-wasting rent seeking. But there are more rudimentary, ethical issues to be addressed.

First, there is the matter of in-period discrimination. It is tautological that government credit programs favor 'targeted sectors' and, *pari passu*, 'targeted', individual beneficiaries. Second, there is the matter of intertemporal discrimination. Reduced to its essentials, government credit programs assist current beneficiaries at the expense of future generations. At the end of fiscal year 1999 the future cost of outstanding direct and guaranteed loans was estimated to be $84 billion. In the case of direct loans, these future costs reflect 'financing account allowance for subsidy cost and the liquidating account allowance for estimated uncollectible principal and interest'. For their part, 'Loan guarantee future costs are estimated liabilities for loan guarantees' (Office of Management and Budget, *Analytical Perspectives*, 2001, Table 8.1, p. 161). Whatever else is said, these 'estimated future costs' are imposed, without their consent, on *future* taxpayers.

The issue of immediate interest is neither the alleged 'Paretian efficiency' of government credit programs nor the political efficiency of a generality constraint. Nor is it the ontological existence of a supraindividual 'social purpose', or the implicit deployment of the 'benevolent despot' model of government. The central issue is the in-period and intergenerational discrimination inherent in government credit programs. The intergenerational discriminatory component of such programs is, in an important sense, decisive: Because the agreement of future generations cannot, by definition, be secured, members of the current and future generations are not temporally equivalent. Granting this, the moral equivalence of persons demands that government credit programs be constitutionally prohibited – whatever their avowed 'social purpose'.

## 9.4 GENERALITY AND GOVERNMENT BORROWING

The financing of government outlay by borrowing rather than taxation has become commonplace. The experience of the United States is heuristic.

United States' budget law distinguishes between on- and off-budget accounts. Social Security and the Postal Service are 'off-budget', with 'on-budget' understood to mean all revenue and outlay programs 'not legally designated as off-budget' (Office of Management and Budget, *A Citizen's Guide to the Federal Budget*, 2001, p. 33).

This on- and off-budget distinction is of particular interest. During the period 1946 to 2000 the federal government's on-budget accounts have been in deficit in all but seven years (Office of Management and Budget, *Historical Tables*, 2001, pp. 23–24). In contrast, the off-budget accounts – essentially Social Security payroll tax proceeds net of Social Security disbursements – have been in surplus in all but eleven years (pp. 23–24).

With this as background, much attention has focused on the emergence of a Unified Budget surplus. The latter, understood to be 'the presentation of the Federal budget in which revenues from all sources and outlays to all activities are consolidated',[7] aggregates on- and off-budget revenues and outlays.

While the on- and off-budget distinction may be operationally important, the Unified Budget concept has particular political significance. Consider first that more than 75 per cent of the projected Unified Budget surplus for the years 2002–2011 consists in a net inflow of Society Security payroll tax receipts (Office of Management and Budget, *Budget*, 2001, Table 5-3, p. 225). It is plausible to assume that the 'representative' taxpayer is unaware that the Social Security surplus which, by law, is to be deposited in a 'trust fund' has, and will, be used for other purposes.[8]

This particular casuistry aside, the issue of immediate concern is the temporal character of government borrowing. As Buchanan and Congleton have emphasized, the purpose of government borrowing 'is to implement the temporal transposition of value – to postpone until later periods the burden of payment for current outlay' (1998, p. 100). This political discrimination against future taxpayers by in-period majorities is clearly violative of the generality principle.

While it is acknowledged that public capital investment projects may yield intertemporal benefits as well as costs, neither this nor the idea of Ricardian equivalence justifies temporal discrimination.[9] The moral equivalence of persons demands that those who cannot agree to bear the future costs of debt-financed government programs be treated impartially. If the institutional imperative is, therefore, a constitutional balanced budget constraint,[10] the same might be said of debt retirement:

> Why should any particular generation of taxpayers be singled out for differentially high taxation, without corresponding benefits, in order to reduce the tax obligations of all persons who will make up the membership of future generations? The generality principle emerges here as a relatively powerful argument against any policy of debt retirement. The 'sins of the past'...should be borne equally across all generations (Buchanan and Congleton 1998, p. 102).

## 9.5 GENERALITY AND REDISTRIBUTION

Governments tend, *ceteris paribus*, to allocate increasing shares of their outlays to transfer programs. The United States experience is, again, heuristic. During fiscal year 1967 means tested entitlements accounted for 3.9 percent of outlays, while Medicare and Social Security represented, respectively, 1.6 and 13.5 percent of total outlays. By fiscal year 2000 outlays on these budget categories accounted, respectively, for 12.7, 10.85 and 22.7 percent of total outlays (Office of Management and Budget, *Historical Tables*, 2001, pp. 125, 127 and 22).[11]

Let us first stipulate that, while Buchanan and Congleton argue that even the generality constrained median voter[12] 'is likely to exhibit bias in favor of transfers over public goods financing', so that 'The inclusive budget will tend to be relatively small in its financing of genuinely public goods and relatively large in its financing of direct transfers' (1998, p. 119), this is not my immediate concern. Neither does my interest center on the rent seeking that is endemic to transfer systems. I simply take as given that the existence of such programs provides incentive both to invest in efforts to qualify for transfers, and to deploy 'public-interest' arguments to justify entitlements.[13] Finally, I acknowledge, without further comment, that 'donors' – those who do not receive transfer payments – may be other-regarding; that they may derive utility from income and other transfers to recipients.[14]

While these considerations, individually and collectively, are important, my fundamental concern is the idea which animates this entire enterprise. As has been repeatedly emphasized, the moral equivalence of persons demands that just, in the sense of impartial, institutions be promoted. On this account it is not the political inefficiency of transfer programs which, while undeniable, is decisive. Rather, it is that transfer programs – excepting, in one sense, those to 'the old' – are inherently discriminatory.[15] Granting this, the logic of 'means testing' is unavailing. The point is not that means testing itself provides incentive for rent seeking (Buchanan and Congleton 1998, pp. 120–121). It is that means testing is itself discriminatory.

Given the moral equivalence of persons, the propensity to affect income and other transfers, and the bias toward discrimination inherent in conflictual, majoritarian politics, the institutional imperative is clear: Insofar as transfer or redistribution programs are to be financed through general tax revenues, a constitutional generality constraint would contemplate 'a flat tax on all income combined with a set of equal-per-head demogrants' (Buchanan and Congleton 1998, p. 118).[16]

If the moral equivalence of persons demands that in-period transfers be generality constrained, transfers from the currently employed to the retired must be subjected to a constitutional, intertemporal generality constraint. As has been suggested, the brute fact that all persons age assures that, in a limited sense, the generality principle is satisfied. That said, both political and 'technical' considerations militate against the impartial treatment of morally equivalent, retired persons. On the one hand, the retired person is subject to the inclinations of successive median voters, especially those who, under pay-as-you-go public pension programs, must absorb the cost of intergenerational transfers. On the other hand, changing birth rates and improvements in medical technology may exert upward pressure on tax rates, and downward pressure on retirement benefits. Taken together, these considerations suggest the possibility of 'majoritarian distributional conflict'. *Inter alia*, 'means testing becomes politically attractive because it reduces the financial claims on the system' (Buchanan and Congleton 1998, p. 127). Reduced to its essentials, the 'generality of aging' aside, the majoritarian impulse toward temporal discrimination applies, *mutatis mutandis*, to public retirement programs. Granting this, 'Intertemporal programs have to ensure equal treatment through time if they are to satisfy the generality principle. This implies that, once enacted, essentially they become permanent' (Buchanan and Congleton 1998, p. 124). The irremediable fact is, however, that demographic and technological changes militate against the constitutionalization of an immutable tax-benefit structure. In the circumstances,

> Effective constitutionalization would suggest that tax rates (or age for eligibility) move upward if the ratio tilts unexpectedly toward a higher number of prospective retirees because of increased life expectancy and that transfer payments move downward if the ratio tilts because of declines in birth rates. Such a rule would violate intergenerational generality but would preserve the fiscal viability of the public pension system (pp. 126–127).

The essential idea is that, under the circumstances envisioned, a constitutional rule, rather than the vagaries of post-constitutional, majoritarian politics animates the requisite programmatic changes.

## 9.6 GENERALITY AND SOCIAL INSURANCE

As was suggested in § 9.3, governments engage in risk underwriting activities. In the United States, the federal government 'insures bank, thrift, and credit union deposits up to $100,000, guarantees private defined-benefit pensions, and insures against other risks such as natural disasters' (Office of Management and Budget, *Analytical Perspectives*, 2001, p. 139). With the 'role' of both its credit and insurance programs characterized as 'helping disadvantaged groups and correcting market failures', the presumption is that such programs can be justified by the presence of 'market imperfections' including information opaqueness, externalities, resource constraints and imperfect competition (pp. 139–140 and 143–144).[17]

While the avowed presence of 'market imperfections' does not, in any case, suggest that the government can 'do better' (§ 5.2), the issue of immediate interest is the moral imperative to manage government insurance programs impartially.

It is appropriate first to acknowledge that 'ex post differentiation is the nature of all true insurance programs' (Buchanan and Congleton 1998, p. 132). This follows from the fact that program benefits depend upon the occurrence of random, future events. What is important, from the generality perspective, is that insurance programs' expected benefits be uniformly distributed among the electorate in an *ex ante* sense. In effect, the requirement is that 'each insured contingency is equally likely, and equally valued, by all within the polity of interest' (p. 132).

Let us first stipulate that adherence to the generality principle is difficult in this setting. First, majoritarian cycling is likely to center on questions of probabilities of occurrence of random events, insurance benefits, and tax prices. Second, as is the case with flood and crop insurance – both provided by the United States government – expected benefits are likely to be concentrated in particular, local polities. Finally, differential degrees of risk aversion imply, *ceteris paribus*, that 'insurance programs that are actuarially identical across individuals may, nonetheless, yield different expected net benefits for more or less risk-averse individuals' (p. 133).

With this as background, we observe that, in the United States, in addition to flood and crop insurance, the federal government insures bank, savings association and credit union deposits, and defined-benefit pension plans. While deposit insurance appears roughly, in the *ex ante* sense, to satisfy the generality principle, the same cannot be said of defined-benefit pension plans, flood or crop insurance.

Given the increasing dominance of defined-contribution pension plans, the defined-benefit 'pension guarantees' proffered by the federal government are both anachronistic and discriminatory.[18] Because all members of the polity do not participate in defined-benefit pension plans – indeed, many individuals have access neither to defined-benefit nor defined-contribution plans – satisfaction of the *ex ante* generality constraint appears beyond reach. Granting this, the impartiality imperative suggests that 'targeted' pension guarantees cannot be justified.

What, then, might be said of what the United States government characterizes as 'disaster insurance'; in particular, flood and crop insurance? It is clear on *a priori* grounds that the benefits of these government-sponsored insurance programs accrue to particular, localized members of the polity.

In the case of flood insurance, the federal government stipulates that 'The number of enrolled policies grew from 2.4 to 4.3 million between 1990 and 2000, and by nearly 82,000 policies in 2001'. Indeed, by 2002 the government's program of subsidized premiums 'is projected to have approximately 4.5 million policies from more than 19,000 communities with $610 billion of insurance in force' (Office of Management and Budget, *Analytical Perspectives*, 2001, p. 158). For its part, 'Subsidized Federal crop insurance administered by the [United States Department of Agriculture] assists farmers in managing yield shortfalls due to bad weather or other natural disasters' (p. 159).[19] This 'crop insurance' coverage has been supplemented, through a pilot program, by an 'Adjusted Gross Revenue (AGR) policy [which] insures the five-year average revenue of a farming or ranching operation on the basis of the producers' Schedule "F" Farm Income on Federal tax returns, instead of its yield history' (p. 159).

Given the 'targeted' nature of flood and crop insurance it is clear that the generality standard cannot be met at the *federal* government level. The expected benefits cannot, in the crucial *ex ante* sense, be uniformly distributed among the national polity. That said, it is also clear that

> Some [government] services that fail to be sufficiently general at a more inclusive level of membership in political community may be acceptable at less inclusive levels of government or within smaller self-financing and autonomous service districts. A federalized structure of government can provide heterogeneous services while satisfying the strictures of generality (Buchanan and Congleton 1998, p. 137).

While this discussion is animated by a normative evaluation of central government 'disaster insurance' programs, the point to be emphasized is generic: 'federal systems may be said to be a first-best institutional arrangement that produces outcomes that cannot be replicated even by an idealized democratic central government' (p. 137).[20] The key idea is that the moral equivalence of persons – and political efficiency – demands that, when *ex ante* expected benefits cannot be uniformly distributed, the constitution prohibit central government goods or service provision. Implicit in this construction is a constitutional federal system under which 'a significant fraction of local government services – or at least pivotal services such as education, transport, and police protection – come to be provided in accordance with the generality principle in the long run' (p. 141).[21] On the one hand, given the constitutional constraint, when expected benefits cannot be uniformly distributed among all members of the national polity, beneficiaries cannot shift service provision to the federal government. On the other hand, given Tiebout-type mobility, competition among political jurisdictions would seem to ensure that 'local governments should be observed widely to provide substantially uniform service packages to all their citizens' (p. 141).

## 9.7 GENERALITY, MARKET INTERVENTIONS AND GENERALIZED EXTERNALITIES

Much of the discussion in § 5.2 centers on the idea that the first fundamental welfare theorem is often deployed to rationalize government intervention in domestic markets. It was shown that, even if one grants the existence of the efficiency frontier, there can be no presumption that, in the presence of 'market failures', the government can do better. That said, once allowance is made for fundamental features of observable reality, the efficiency frontier is rendered indeterminate (Chapter 6). Granting this, government market intervention motivated by the familiar Paretian efficiency or welfare conditions must be regarded as *ad hoc*. A central message of this book is, therefore, that the logic of the Paretian efficiency standard cannot justify government market intervention.

There is a sense, however, in which in many cases of practical importance the logical, empirical and ontological problems associated with the first and second fundamental welfare theorems are irrelevant.[22] I have in mind government interventions in domestic and international markets motivated by political rather than 'scientific' considerations. These politically motivated interventions are the subject of §§ 9.71 and 9.72. For its part, § 9.73 revisits the problem of generalized externalities. Whereas § 5.2 focused, *inter alia*, on the 'measurement' of private and social cost, § 9.73 concentrates upon what might be characterized as the 'legal environment'. At issue is the external and internal morality of 'environmental' law.

### 9.71 Generality and Internal Market Interventions

It is useful again to emphasize that the domestic market interventions of interest here are those which cannot be 'justified' by appeal to departures from 'first-best Paretian optimality'. While much of the excludable goods discussion in § 9.32 has basic relevance, the focus here is upon what has come to be characterized as 'government regulation'.

Once again, the exposition is facilitated by appeal to the United States' experience. Examples of politically motivated regulatory interventions in labor and product markets abound: The Davis-Bacon Act requires that workers employed on construction projects involving federal government funding be paid the 'prevailing' – effectively, union – wage. While obviously consonant with the interests of 'organized labor', it also insulates unionized contractors from competitive pressures. The Clean Air Act of 1990, while animated by environmental concerns, enhances the market prospects of corn farmers and producers of natural gas and power-plant scrubbers (Gutfeld 1990). For their part, United States Department of Agriculture 'marketing orders' make it a federal crime for California farmers to sell nectarines less than 2-3/8 inches in diameter (Bovard 1992). While its 'nectarine policy' is predicated on the claim that 'larger sized nectarines provide greater consumer satisfaction than those of smaller sizes', the Department provides no supporting evidence. In any case, the practical effect of such marketing orders is to increase the price of fruit.[23]

Whatever else is said, such 'regulations' – often obscure and frequently arcane – inure to the benefit of well-defined constituencies, and disperse the essentially hidden costs across affected consumers.

While the concentrated benefit-dispersed cost phenomenon is a catalyst to the promulgation of both 'economic' and 'social regulations'[24] and 'mandated benefits',[25] another force is at work. The essential idea is that regulatory activity is animated, in part, by what has been characterized as an institutional overclaiming problem. The problem is that '[a] lobby can go to the...legislature and say, "Let us have our way. You're not going to have to pay for this"' (Epstein 1992, p. 9).[26]

It is tautological that rent seeking – here, the 'demand for regulation' – accounts for the politically motivated regulatory impulse.[27] So strong is this impulse that, in 1979, the congressional Joint Economic Committee, a non-legislative body, recommended promulgation of a Regulatory Budget. Of particular interest is the Committee's invocation of 'off-off-budget' spending or 'the costs of compliance with Federal regulations' (U.S. Congress Joint Economic Committee, 1979, pp. 53–54). Although it never became law, the Regulatory Budget was intended to 'set a limit on the costs of compliance each agency could impose on the private sector' (p. 53). Then, in 1981, President Reagan issued Executive Order No. 12291 which requires that the Office of Management and Budget 'Develop procedures for estimating the annual benefits and costs of agency regulations, on an aggregate and economic or industrial sector basis, for purposes of compiling a regulatory budget'.[28]

We now know that efforts to deploy an 'economic analysis' of regulations have been systematically ignored.[29] Setting aside the technical and other problems associated with the measurement of regulatory benefits and costs, a statutory solution to the concentrated benefit-dispersed cost problem is, in any case, unavailing. *Inter alia,* 'no Congress can bind a succeeding Congress by a simple statue' (United States Senate, Committee on the Judiciary, 1981, p. 42). There is, in short, no assurance that a statutory restraint would eliminate, or even mitigate, politically motivated regulatory activity.

Granting this, it is possible to make a political efficiency case for a constitutional restraint on politically motivated regulation. While the argument is persuasive, there is a sense in which it misses the point.

Let us be clear. This discussion is animated by 'interferences with domestic trade that cannot be justified, on any honest evaluation, on the basis of either externality or public goods arguments' (Buchanan and Congleton 1998, p. 77). At issue, therefore, are explicitly discriminatory policies intended to benefit well-defined constituencies at others' expense. Given the moral equivalence of persons, this is plainly unacceptable, and should be constitutionally prohibited.

## 9.72 Generality and External Market Interventions

As is well known, producers of import substitutes have incentive to seek 'protection' from foreign competition. What is perhaps less well known is that exporters are also rent seekers. In the United States this impulse finds statutory expression in programs institutionalized by the federal government:

> Seven Federal agencies, the Department of Agriculture (USDA), the Department of Defense, the Department of State, the Department of the Treasury, the Agency for International Development (AID), the Export-Import Bank, and the Overseas Private Investment Corporation (OPIC), provide direct loans, loan guarantees, and insurance to a variety of foreign private and sovereign borrowers. These programs are intended to level the playing field for U.S. exporters, deliver robust support for U.S. manufactured goods, stabilize international financial markets, and promote sustainable development (Office of Management and Budget, *Analytical Perspectives*, 2001, pp. 154–155).[30]

On the not implausible assumption that import restraints and export subsidies are not motivated by departures from first-best Paretian optimality, government interventions in external markets must be understood to be the result of intendedly discriminatory rent seeking activity.[31] In short, even if one were to grant its normative value, the Paretian efficiency standard has no immediate relevance.

Whatever else is said, the political inefficiency inherent in external market interventions argues for appeal to a generality constraint. But more is at issue. As has been repeatedly emphasized, the moral equivalence of persons implies an imperative to promote just, in the sense of impartial, institutions. In the instant case, the body of 'trade law' must be nondiscriminatory.[32]

Consider, for example, the question of import restraints. While a uniform tariff rate imposed on all imports may, on first inspection, appear to be impartial, in fact it would be discriminatory. *Inter alia*, 'it discriminates overtly against those producing interests that seek only to enter exchanges in domestic markets or to sell to foreigners. And any such market restriction also discriminates against persons in their roles as consumers' (Buchanan and Congleton 1998, p. 80). It is, of course, transparent that export subsidies discriminate against producers that sell only in domestic markets. Moreover, direct and guaranteed loans to foreign private and sovereign borrowers impose indirect and, in the event of defaults, direct costs on taxpayers, most of whom have no equity or other interest in the export-subsidized enterprises.

Granting the logic of what has been said, the moral equivalence of persons demands a constitutional prohibition against politically motivated external market interventions. Absent such a constitutional constraint the presumption must be that post-constitutional 'trade law' would violate both the external and the internal morality of law (§ 8.2).

### 9.73 Generality and Generalized Externalities

Intendedly discriminatory market intervention is inconsistent with the moral equivalence of persons. This is true whether the intervention is 'politically motivated', as in §§ 9.71 and 9.72, or it is animated by the presence of generalized externalities (§ 5.2).

There is, however, a fundamental difference between the two decision environments. In the first, the objective is to concentrate benefits among well-defined constituencies while dispersing costs across all taxpayers. In the second, the intent is to institutionalize use-right assignments, regulations and sanctions so as to secure Pareto optimal outcomes.

While the indeterminacy of the efficiency frontier (Chapter 6) calls into question the normative use of the Paretian efficiency standard, it seems clear that divergences between private and social cost will continue to animate 'environmental' and other policies. This is true, moreover, despite the conceptual and empirical difficulties associated with these concepts (§ 5.2).

Granting this, it is important to acknowledge the political efficiency case for a generality constraint on environment law: Asymmetric treatment – whatever its nature – of different sources of identical effluents 'open[s] environmental law up to the machinations of majoritarian politics and special interest groups while increasing enforcement and adherence costs' (Buchanan and Congleton 1998, p. 65).[33] That said, it is also clear that, *in principle*, the political efficiency gains attributable to an operative generality constraint may be offset by reductions in Paretian efficiency. While this is less likely in the case of reciprocal externalities, the probability of a political-Paretian efficiency tradeoff is enhanced in the case of nonreciprocal externalities (pp. 65–69).

Given the indeterminacy of the Paretian efficiency standard (Chapter 6), the potential tradeoff should not, in any case, be decisive. Moreover, the case for generality is enhanced when account is taken of intertemporal phenomena:

> in cases in which technological or other changes affect the payoffs of externality generating activities or create new unanticipated possibilities, the ideal pattern, range and domain of use rights change through time, often in ways that cannot be anticipated. So long as political decisions have to be reached on such matters, there remains an important role for the generality principle as a guide to policy formation (Buchanan and Congleton 1998, p. 75).

If political efficiency justifies appeal to a constitutional generality constraint on environmental law, the external morality of law demands it. From the Kantian/Rawlsian contractarian perspective – the perspective which informs this book – the moral equivalence of persons demands that the greatest possible equal liberty be promoted, and that institutions be impartial. On this account, constraints on behavior – like those contemplated by environmental law – must fall equally upon all persons (§§ 7.4 and 8.2). *Inter alia*, the constitution must require that all sources of identical effluents be treated equally.

## 9.8 THE LEGISLATIVE PROCESS AND THE MORALITY OF LAW

The relationship between the generality principle and the rule of law is the subject of § 8.2. Emphasis is placed on the idea that the principle of equal liberty – or of equal participation when applied to the political procedure defined by the constitution – finds its normative foundation in the moral equivalence of persons. Following Rawls (1971), distinctions are drawn among the meaning, extent and worth or value of equal political participation.

Given that the external morality of law demands that the greatest possible equal political participation be promoted, the meaning, extent and value of the latter are of immediate and central concern. That said, because the value of equal political participation is of particular importance to postconstitutional, majoritarian politics, it is important again to emphasize that 'the constitution must take steps to enhance the value of the equal rights of participation for all members of society' (Rawls 1971, p. 224). *Inter alia*, the constitution must both 'underwrite a fair opportunity to take part in and to influence the political process' (p. 224), and ensure that all citizens 'have the means to be informed about political issues' (p. 225).

While these constitutional imperatives inform the balance of this section, so too does Rawls's 'summing up' of the 'account of the principle of participation':

> The principle of [equal] participation compels those in authority to be responsive to the felt interests of the electorate. Representatives are not, to be sure, mere agents of their constituents, since they have a certain discretion and they are expected to exercise their judgment in enacting legislation. In a well-ordered society they must, nevertheless, represent their constituents in the substantive sense: they must first seek to pass just and effective legislation, since this is a citizen's first interest in government, and secondly, they must further their constituents' other interests insofar as these are consistent with justice.... When the principle of [equal] participation is satisfied, all have the common status of equal citizen (1971, p. 227).

Reduced to its essentials, the moral equivalence of persons and, *mutatis mutandis*, the principle of equal political participation, implies both constitutional and post-constitutional imperatives. At the constitutional stage, 'equal citizens' must be ensured both of a fair opportunity to take part in and to influence the political process and to be informed about political issues. Then, at the post-constitutional stage, their elected representatives must pass just, in the sense of impartial, legislation.

Given these institutional imperatives the 'legislative process' becomes a subject of normative appraisal. As before, discussion is facilitated by appeal to the United States' experience; in particular, by an evaluation of the recent legislative history of the United States Congress.

Let us first stipulate that voters are boundedly rational (Chapter 6). *Inter alia*, cognitive limitations on receiving, storing, retrieving, and processing information impel voters to partition interrelated issues. This, in turn, gives their elected representatives wide discretion over the legislative actions taken (Kuran 1991, pp. 242 and 252–253). For example, a 'voluntary restraint agreement' on 'illegally subsidized' flat-rolled foreign steel products may be regarded by voters as both 'fair' and costless. Yet, insofar as it results in an increase in the price of automobiles and other durable goods, the 'voluntary restraint agreement' is not costless. Their elected representatives may, nevertheless, secure support for intendedly discriminatory trade restraints based on voters' failure to appreciate the implications of the 'fair' and 'costless' policy intervention. Under the circumstances voter 'oversight' is unavailing, and the case for a generality constraint is once again apparent.

Absent a generality constraint, voters' propensity to partition issues renders them vulnerable to the rent seeking activities of 'special interests'. Yet, if voters may be exploited because they are boundedly rational, institutional 'logrolling' compounds the problem.

To see this, consider first that legislators representing 'special interests' can 'rarely succeed on their own':

> for any measure or set of measures devised through negotiation and exchange, there exists another measure that will command a majority against it. No [legislative initiative benefiting one interest] is invulnerable to an alternative proposal...no legislative exchange in an unstructured legislature is self-enforcing (Weingast 1991, p. 263).

Like other legislative bodies, the United States Congress has sought to resolve this problem by creating some 200 committees and subcommittees, each with jurisdiction over a subset of policy 'issues' (Ornstein, Mann and Malbin 2000, Table 4-2). These committees have 'gate keeping power' (Weingast 1991, p. 265) over the initiation of legislation. Moreover, by virtue of their specialized 'institutional knowledge', or human capital specificity,[34] committee members have a comparative advantage relative to other members of Congress. In short, committee members do not simply initiate legislation; they shape the information which flows to the rest of the Congress. That said, all committees have a common problem: How does a committee command the support of a majority when its legislation comes before the 'entire body', whether the House or the Senate?

The solution is bundling legislation. Typically, language designed to benefit 'targeted' congressional districts or 'special interests' is inserted in 'omnibus' bills whose sheer volume and arcane legislative language make them unintelligible to voters. While bundling legislation facilitates 'logrolling' it clearly compounds the voters' information asymmetry problem. On the one hand, bundling legislation solves a congressional enforcement problem. Because reneging on agreements to support each others' projects would doom the entire bill, individual legislators with 'targeted' interests have the incentive to support the entire omnibus measure. On the other hand, the *ex ante* and *ex post* costs of monitoring omnibus appropriations, tax and other bills are, from the perspective of the individual voter, prohibitively high. Indeed, on two accounts, the same might be said of Members of Congress and their staffs:

> On September 30, 1996 Congress passed a 2,000 page, 17-pound bill appropriating almost $400 billion and adding several new criminal offenses to the federal statute books. Sen. Robert Byrd of West Virginia complained, 'I dare say no staff person has had time to carefully review the thousands of programs funded in this resolution, or to read and comprehend the many nonappropriations, legislative matters contained in this resolution'.... Sen. Jim Inhofe of Oklahoma said, 'I would suggest there is not one Member of this body who has read this [2000-plus page] bill' (Bovard 1999, pp. 110–111).

An account of the passage of a 1991 highway bill suggests a somewhat less benign interpretation of Members' failure to read the legislation upon which they vote:

> Members [of Congress] may not have been given a chance to see the bill after the conferees were done with it, but they didn't care. Each member knew there would be some road, bridge, tunnel, sidewalk, bus or subway earmarked for his home district.... Around 2:00 a.m. November 27, the bill was taken up by the House Rules Committee.... At 4:00 a.m., debate began – though no one had yet seen the bill. Not until nearly 5:00 a.m., halfway through the debate, was one copy of the document plunked down on the Speaker's table on the House floor. There it sat until 6:00 a.m., when the vote was taken. 372 for, 47 against – not a single member had read it.[35]

If one grants, as I do, that these anecdotes are broadly descriptive of observable reality, the 'legislative process', as it unfolds in both chambers of the United States Congress, is violative of the principle of equal participation and, *pari passu*, of the moral equivalence of persons.

There is no sense in which the legislative process just described embodies a 'fair opportunity to take part in and to influence the political process'. Nor, in the circumstances, can it legitimately be claimed that all citizens 'have the means to be informed about political issues'. And, finally, there is no sense in which Members of Congress can be construed to be seeking to pass just, in the sense of impartial, legislation. Simply stated, the legislative process denies voters their right, as morally equivalent 'equal citizens', to equal political participation. It follows, *pari passu*, that the laws which emerge from the legislative process violate the external morality of law. This is true, moreover, of the internal morality of the law. Of particular interest is the precept that laws should be promulgated or made known to those to whom they apply (§ 8.2). It is after all clear that laws which are not comprehensively apprehended by legislators are likely not to be comprehended in their entirety by all affected parties.

Given rent seeking and the inability of any Congress to constrain the actions of subsequent Congresses, a statutory solution is unavailable. If the moral equivalence of persons and their right to equal political participation are to be respected, the constitution must be amended. While a constitutional generality constraint cannot plausibly contemplate either an *a priori* limit on the number of committees and subcommittees or a prohibition against 'logrolling', it can require, in the spirit of earlier discussion, that all legislation respect the external and internal morality of law. *Inter alia*, this would contemplate a constitutional prohibition against 'omnibus' or bundling legislation.[36]

Finally, it must be acknowledged that rights carry with them correlative duties. In the instant case, justice as impartiality implies a 'duty of justice'.

This duty 'requires us to support and to comply with just institutions that exist and apply to us. It also constrains us to further just arrangements not yet established, at least when this can be done without too much cost to ourselves' (Rawls 1971, p. 115).[37]

While the duty of justice can be construed in many ways, it seems clear that citizens have a duty both to engage in constitutional discourse and to promote the constitutionalization of a generality constraint, *inter alia*, on the legislative process. Then, in the post-constitutional stage, the duty of justice seems to me to imply an obligation to monitor the legislative process.

Granting this, morally equivalent citizens possessed of a right to equal political participation have a duty to 'stay informed'. Yet, having surveyed a body of evidence, James Bovard concludes that 'If citizen comprehension of government and public affairs is the currency of democracy, America is long since bankrupt' (1999, p. 105).[38] According to Bovard,

> The issue is not whether a viable democracy can survive an unlimited level of government complexity. Obviously, at some point, there will be so much on the public-agenda plate that even conscientious citizens are overwhelmed. The question is, has America reached that point yet? Or, perhaps more importantly, has America already reached that point for sufficient numbers of voters that elections are turned into mere contests of demagoguery and bathos? (p. 109).

While it is not possible constitutionally to ensure that morally equivalent persons will respect their duty to 'further just arrangements not yet established', it is clear that their right to equal political participation, the political inefficiency of post-constitutional majoritarian politics and the bounded rationality of citizens argue for a constitutional generality constraint on the legislative process. Whatever else is said, the constraint must contemplate a prohibition against 'omnibus' or bundling legislation.

## NOTES

1. In the peculiar vernacular of the *Budget of the United States Government*, such 'preferential provisions' are referred to as 'tax expenditures'. This characterization of preferential tax code provisions reflects 'the notion that the Federal Government would otherwise collect additional revenues but for these provisions' (Office of Management and Budget, *Analytical Perspectives*, 2001, p. 61). For estimates of tax expenditures by fiscal year, see *Analytical Perspectives*, 2001, Chapter 5.
2. Social Security and Railroad Retirement, Federal Employees Retirement Insurance, Unemployment Assistance, Medical Care, Assistance to Students, Housing Assistance, Food and Nutrition Assistance, Public Assistance and Related Programs and All Other Payments for Individuals fall under the rubric of Payments for Individuals. See Office of Management and Budget, *Historical Tables*, 2001, p. 215.
3. In addition to direct transfer payments, the United States government provides 'other safety-net protections, such as the marketing assistance loans that guarantee a minimum

price for major commodities, which paid producers $7 billion in 2000 and will pay them about $6 billion in 2001' (Office of Management and Budget, *Budget*, 2001, p. 55). Such loans are the subject matter of § 9.33.

4. It is interesting that United States and international trade law establish the illegality of such 'trade promotion' activities as 'dumping'. Presumably, 'dumping' – the sale of products at prices below those charged in home markets – is sometimes (frequently?) facilitated by home government subsidies. In any case, the expected cost of a constitutional generality constraint to treat all producers equally – whether through direct subsidies, direct loans or loan guarantees – would likely be regarded as prohibitively expensive. Granting this, argument at the constitutional stage would likely contemplate a prohibition against all such taxpayer-financed activities.
5. See, especially, Office of Management and Budget, *Analytical Perspectives*, 2001, p. 139.
6. Government-sponsored enterprises include the Federal National Mortgage Association and the Farm Credit Banks. Established by the federal government, they 'provide financial intermediation for specific public purposes. They are excluded from the budget because they are privately owned and controlled. However, primarily because they were established by the Federal Government for public policy purposes, estimates of their activity are reported in a separate chapter of the budget Appendix' (Office of Management and Budget, *Analytical Perspectives*, 2001, p. 333).
7. Office of Management and Budget, *A Citizen's Guide to the Federal Budget*, 2001, p. 34.
8. Indeed, federal law requires that Social Security and other trust fund balances be invested in Treasury debt securities (Office of Management and Budget, *Analytical Perspectives*, 2001, p. 304). The record shows, however, that this has not been done.
9. *Inter alia*, future period tax sources could be earmarked to service and amortize specific investment project-related costs (Buchanan and Congleton 1998, p. 101; see also pp. 99–100).
10. Again, allowance could, in principle, be made for public investment projects. See footnote 9. It should be recognized, however, that it is sometimes difficult to distinguish between 'investment' and 'consumption'. Granting this, a constitutional balanced budget constraint which is 'appropriately adjusted to allow for special treatment for public investment projects' (Buchanan and Congleton 1998, p. 101) may open the door both to in-period and temporal rent seeking. For more on this balanced budget–public investment debate, see Peletier, Dur and Swank (1999).
11. The data begin, for present purposes, in 1967 because Medicare disbursements began in that year. 'Means tested entitlements' include Medicaid, food stamps, family support assistance, supplemental security income, child nutrition programs and earned income tax credits (Office of Management and Budget, *Historical Tables*, 2001, p. 125, fn 1). Medicare is 'a nationwide health insurance program for the elderly and certain people with disabilities', while Social Security 'provides monthly benefits to retired and disabled workers who gain insured status and to their eligible spouses, children, and survivors' (Office of Management and Budget, *Budget*, 2001, pp. 105 and 115).
12. Here, generality connotes flat-rate income tax financed equal-per-head demogrants.
13. In Buchanan and Congleton's account, in a setting in which the franchise is not limited to those who pay net taxes, 'As the population of recipients increases relative to that of nonrecipients, majoritarian politics tends to shift transfer levels [to the poor] further from those acceptable to net taxpayers, thereby exacerbating political tension and increasing the potential for class conflict' (1998, p. 122).
14. It should also be acknowledged that some 'donors' may care about the consumption patterns of income transfer recipients. This may, in part, account for the emergence of in-kind transfer programs.
15. As Buchanan and Congleton have suggested, because all persons 'get old', 'all persons are eventually eligible for program benefits' (1998, p. 122). In this sense, then, the generality or impartiality principle is satisfied.
16. The equal-per-head demogrants would extend to the direct or subsidized provision of in-kind services such as medical care. That said, it should be recognized that pressures for departure from generality will emanate both from prospective beneficiaries and service

providers. While these pressures will likely always be present, 'genuine constitutionalization of all such in-kind programs can be helpful in attenuating the potential distributional conflict' (Buchanan and Congleton 1998, p. 125).

17. In the United States the Department of Labor also manages an unemployment insurance program. Styled 'Unemployment Compensation' the program 'provides benefits to individuals who are temporarily out of work through no fault of their own and whose employer has previously paid payroll taxes to the program' (Office of Management and Budget, *Budget*, 2001, p. 112). Whatever else is said, the employer-driven eligibility requirement is clearly violative of the generality principle.
18. The United States government acknowledges that 'The number of plans insured...has been declining as small companies with defined-benefit plans terminate them and shift to defined-contribution pension arrangements'. Indeed, the number of active workers in defined-benefit plans fell from 29 million in 1985 to fewer than 24 million in 1995. The federal government concludes that, 'If the trend continues, by 2003 fewer than half of the participants in defined-benefit plans will be active workers; the rest will be retirees' (Office of Management and Budget, *Analytical Perspectives*, 2001, p. 157).
19. In fact, the United States government does not simply subsidize farmers' insurance premiums. It also 'reimburses private [insurance] companies for the administrative expenses associated with providing crop insurance and reinsures the private companies for excess insurance losses on all policies' (Office of Management and Budget, *Analytical Perspectives*, 2001, p. 159).
20. In the United States the federal system contemplates the national or federal government, fifty state governments and, within states, counties, townships and cities. Within this structure, taxing and spending decisions are contingent, at each 'level' of government, upon the government services provided. For a discussion of the evolution of local, state and federal financial responsibility in the American setting, see Wallis (2000).
21. It should be noted that, in a federal system, state and local governments may, themselves, engage in a form of rent seeking. See, for example, Mixon and Hobson (2001).
22. For a discussion of the second fundamental welfare theorem, see § 5.3.
23. For other examples of politically motivated regulations, see Bovard (1999, p. 114).
24. For a discussion of the distinction drawn between the two, see Council of Economic Advisers (1989, p. 190).
25. 'Mandated benefits' contemplate employee and other benefits which federal law requires that private sector enterprises provide.
26. For more on the idea that 'social' regulation is an 'increasingly attractive mechanism for redistributing wealth, given fiscal constraints' see Hahn (1998, especially p. 209).
27. It should be clear that, if producers exhibit effective demand for regulation, the same can be said of consumers. Episodic calls for retail gasoline price controls are an example.
28. President Clinton replaced the Reagan Executive Order No. 12291 with Executive Order No. 12886, which requires similar regulatory analyses (Hahn 1998, pp. 202–203).
29. There is, for example, no mention of the benefits and costs of agency regulations in the federal government's Fiscal Year 2002 *Budget*. This is true, moreover, despite an amendment to the Omnibus Consolidated Appropriations Act of 1997 requiring the Director of the Office of Management and Budget to provide Congress with estimates of the total annual benefits and costs of all federal regulatory programs, and estimates of the benefits and costs of individual regulations (Hahn 1998, pp. 201–202).
30. For a discussion of agricultural export subsidy programs, see § 9.32.
31. For opposing views, see Mitra (1999) and Goldberg and Maggi (1999). The authors suggest that, in contrast to the Grossman and Helpman (1994) 'protection for sale' model, 'the government' establishes trade policy, in part, by taking account of 'social welfare'.
32. Of course, it must also reflect the precepts of the internal morality of law (§ 8.2).
33. The same political efficiency argument applies to so-called positive externalities. In the situation envisioned, marginal social costs are lower than marginal private costs. By a familiar line of reasoning, first-best Paretian optimality requires that public policy reduce private costs by the 'Pareto optimal' amount. This logic accounts, *inter alia*, for government subsidy programs intended to promote the development and application of new

technology. It is interesting to note, however, that when government subsidies are either not provided, are withdrawn, or are 'threatened', the private sector sometimes proceeds without government 'assistance'. See, for example, Carey and Kunii (2001).

34. See, for example, Furubotn and Richter (1997, pp. 128–129).
35. Eric Felton, quoted in Bovard (1999, p. 110).
36. It is, of course, understood that 'even the ideal legislature is an imperfect procedure. There seems to be no way to characterize a feasible procedure guaranteed to lead to just legislation' (Rawls 1971, p. 360; see also p. 362).
37. See also Rawls (1971, Chapter 6, especially p. 334).
38. For a discussion of survey, poll and other evidence suggesting, *inter alia*, that '"only 26 percent [of respondents] knew the 6-year term of office of a U.S. Senator" and less than half the public knows that a member of the House of Representatives is elected to a two-year term' see Bovard (1999, pp. 105–109).

# 10. Generality and minimalist government

## 10.1 MAJORITARIAN CYCLING, RENT SEEKING AND THE GROWTH OF GOVERNMENT

If, as John Rawls suggests, a constitutional democracy can be arranged so as to satisfy the principle of equal political participation it is also true that, absent a generality constraint, majoritarian democracy is congenial to discriminatory, resource-wasting rent seeking activity. This brute fact comes into focus once the romanticized view of politics is abandoned. While analytically convenient, neither the 'bifurcated man' nor the 'benevolent despot' has an empirical counterpart. On the one hand, there is no reason to suppose that man is narrowly self-interested in his market behavior, and other-regarding in his political behavior. On the other hand, the notion that 'government' can be modeled as a single entity seeking to maximize a supraindividualistic social welfare function denies both the reality of complex political processes and the ontological and other problems associated with the specification of an externally defined public good.

Reduced to its essentials, majoritarian cycling and rent seeking are endemic to the conflictual or day-to-day political process. The irremediable fact is that objective features of observable reality facilitate the concentration of benefits and the dispersion of costs which, in turn, underwrite the growth of government. *Inter alia*, bounded rationality, positive *ex ante* and *ex post* monitoring costs and opportunism shape a decision environment in which 'special interests' secure the discriminatory in-period and intergenerational transfers which, *pari passu*, imply an expansion of the size and scope of 'government'.

If the political inefficiency inherent in resource-wasting rent seeking provides incentive for appeal to a constitutionally mandated generality constraint, so too does the *ad hoc* deployment of the first and second fundamental welfare theorems. Given the indeterminacy of both the efficiency frontier and the social welfare function, neither perceived market failures nor presumed differences between 'competitive' and 'ethical' equilibria imply the existence of an optimal government intervention.[1] That said, economists' intellectual commitment to outcomes-based, procedurally detached and intendedly value-free social welfare theory accounts for their adherence to the romanticized view of politics. In this account, 'positivist' policy prescriptions inform a 'benevolent despot' who, in turn, affects decisions in an institutional vacuum.

Whatever else is said, it is clear that the economist's theory of the state – effectively summarized by the two fundamental welfare theorems – facilitates the rationalization of all manner of 'government interventions'. Granting the indeterminacy of the efficiency frontier and the social welfare function, these 'interventions' can have no 'scientific' foundation.[2] Moreover, because the theory can accommodate neither the moral force of rights nor any plausible understanding of justice such 'interventions' have no moral basis.

While nothing that has been said suggests that the growth of government is, perforce, 'bad', this much is clear: Majoritarian cycling, rent seeking, and *ad hoc* invocations of the two fundamental welfare theorems both underwrite the growth of government and deny the 'basic principle of collective order, that of equal treatment' (Buchanan [1975] 2000, p. 51).

In a fundamental sense, the 'growth of government' is a lower order issue. While appeal to a generality constraint is 'politically efficient' and would, *pari passu*, limit the growth of government, the imperative to promote just or impartial institutions flows from a prior, ethical commitment to the moral equivalence of persons. The principle of equal liberty, or of equal participation when applied to the political procedure defined by the constitution, finds its normative basis in the same, prior commitment.

## 10.2 THE EXTERNAL AND INTERNAL MORALITY OF GOVERNMENT INSTITUTIONS

If morally equivalent persons are entitled to impartial treatment under and by the law they are also entitled to the greatest possible equal liberty and, *mutatis mutandis*, to equal political participation.

The institutional imperatives to which these ethical predicates give rise have been discussed in detail. I wish only to emphasize that, while these ideas inform the idealized rule of law and, *pari passu*, the work of an idealized, post-constitutional judiciary, a curious, if not anomalous, ethical lacuna has emerged. Given that the external and internal morality of law is grounded in an ethical prior commitment to the moral equivalence of persons one might plausibly ask, What accounts for the failure systematically to apply these ideas to other institutions of post-constitutional or conflictual politics?

Among economists the asymmetry may be traced to their intellectual commitment to utilitarian social welfare theory. On the one hand, because unattenuated property and exchange rights are instrumentally important to the achievement of first-best Paretian optima, the 'rule of law' – in the limited sense of 'rights protection' – is, itself, instrumentally important. On the other hand, this 'truncated' view of the rule of law may be attributed to the inability of utilitarian social welfare theory to accommodate any plausible understanding of justice.[3] Above all, in contrast to Kantian/Rawlsian contractarian theory, consequentialist social welfare theory is not grounded in a prior commitment to the moral equivalence of persons. Indeed, as we have seen, intendedly value-free and procedurally detached social welfare theory can be deployed to rationalize Pareto 'efficiency-enhancing' corruption. Add to this the romanticized view of politics and the single-minded pursuit of Pareto optimal outcomes and it is clear that the rules of the conflictual politics game are beyond the purview of received, consequentialist social welfare theory.

Considered *in vacuo*, the indeterminacy of the efficiency frontier and the social welfare function is debilitating. *Inter alia*, the first and second fundamental welfare theorems cannot meaningfully inform the 'benevolent despot'. In effect, the 'omniscient being – the observing economist' envisioned by Graaff (1957, p. 13) lacks the analytical tools by which to configure 'optimal', outcomes-based public policy. Yet, the indeterminacy of social welfare theory's fundamental theoretical constructs cannot be considered *in vacuo*. Reduced to its essentials, the relentless pursuit of Pareto-optimal outcomes ignores the discriminatory nature of conflictual or day-to-day politics. Stated differently, the economist's theory of the state does not contemplate the external and internal morality of post-constitutional political institutions.

If one accepts, as I do, a prior ethical commitment to the moral equivalence of persons, certain corollaries follow. First, while political inefficiency is important, resource-wasting rent seeking is not the decisive consideration. From the Kantian/Rawlsian perspective, what *is* decisive is that government institutions respect the moral equivalence of persons. Second, because they are inherently discriminatory, majoritarian cycling and rent seeking are immoral. Third, the institutions of post-constitutional governance which facilitate discriminatory treatment are, *pari passu*, immoral.

Granting all of this, the principles which inform the idealized rule of law – its external and internal morality – must also apply to the legislative and executive branches of government. While these principles are adumbrated in § 8.2, the essential idea is that justice – in the sense of impartiality – demands that the generality principle be incorporated both in the rule of law *and* in the constitutional rules of conflictual or day-to-day politics. Moreover, given the lexical priority of rights, the principle of the greatest possible equal liberty, defined by the principle of equal participation, must constrain the post-constitutional political process.

## 10.3 THE GENERALITY PRINCIPLE, THE MORAL EQUIVALENCE OF PERSONS, AND THE SIZE AND SCOPE OF GOVERNMENT

Whereas consequentialist social welfare theory is outcomes-based and procedurally detached, the Kantian/Rawlsian contractarian enterprise which informs this book is procedural. According to this,

> the legitimacy of basic constitutional principles is judged not against some predefined 'ideal system' but in terms of the process from which these principles emerge. The normative focus is on the characteristics of the process of constitutional choice, not on characteristics of choice-outcomes as such. Furthermore,...a 'good' or 'proper' process is defined as one that assures *fairness* or *impartiality* in the rules that emerge (Buchanan 1991, p. 59).

Because normative appraisal is restricted to questions of institutional design, the size and scope of government activity cannot, on contractarian terms, be established *a priori*.[4] That this must be so follows from the fact that, whereas utilitarians can offer only a contingent defense of constitutional democracy, the principle of equal political participation *implies* a constitutional democracy. Granting this, the government activities extant within any polity at any cross-section of time will reflect equally weighted, *individual* assessments of the public good.[5] Yet, whatever fiscal, regulatory, or other post-constitutional programs emerge, the moral equivalence of persons must be respected. *Ceteris paribus*, this constraint will be satisfied if the constitution mandates both the greatest possible equal political participation *and* the impartial treatment of morally equivalent persons.[6]

Properly construed, then, a constitutionally embedded generality constraint does not determine *what* government *at any level* will do. Rather, normative appraisal centers upon *how* government does what it does. This programmatic indeterminacy notwithstanding, it is nevertheless possible to conclude that equal participation-generality constrained conflictual politics would give rise to minimalist government.

The minimalist state envisioned here does not correspond to the libertarian, rights protection construal.[7] It is, of course, true that the Kantian/Rawlsian contractarian enterprise assigns lexical priority to rights. Hence, 'rights protection' – in the sense of the promotion of the greatest possible equal liberty and, *mutatis mutandis*, of the greatest possible equal political participation – is a necessary part of the resultant constitutional agenda. But so, too, is the generality constraint which the moral equivalence of persons demands. Granting this, the probability is enhanced that post-constitutional politics will not be animated by the concentrated benefit-dispersed cost calculus. It is in this sense that a 'minimalist state' would emerge.[8]

If the principle of equal political participation and appeal to a generality constraint would contribute to the emergence of a minimalist state, rejection of the economist's romanticized view of politics would also be instrumentally important. While the 'omniscient economist–benevolent despot' formulation is, itself, palpably absurd, the essential point is that the indeterminacy of the efficiency frontier and the social welfare function militates against the 'scientific' deployment of the first and second fundamental welfare theorems. If, as I have argued, government interventions motivated by the two theorems must therefore be regarded as *ad hoc*, it is also true that these interventions have contributed to the growth of government. Yet, even if the theoretical, empirical and ontological objections to consequentialist social welfare theory were set aside, the implicit presumption that government can, unfailingly, correct market failures has contributed to the growth of government. As Sandmo has suggested,

> In their analyses of the effects of externalities welfare economists may sometimes have fallen into the trap of arguing that if the market fails, the government is sure to do better...thereby making welfare economics and its applications much more progovernment and prointerference than could be justified on scientific grounds (1990, p. 58).[9]

To Sandmo's account I would add only that the same might be said of the second fundamental welfare theorem: Because social welfare theory cannot accommodate any plausible understanding of justice, redistribution schemes motivated by claimed differences between 'competitive' and 'ethical' equilibria cannot be justified on ethical grounds. Rather, they must be understood to be the product of in-period and intergenerational rent seeking.

In sum, the contractarian enterprise of which this book is a part does not contemplate an 'optimal' size or scope of 'government'. Rather, the 'minimalist state' is a corollary of the rejection of the economists' theory of the state, and a prior, ethical commitment to the moral equivalence of persons.

## NOTES

1. The indeterminacy of the Paretian efficiency standard means, *inter alia*, that there is no 'tradeoff' between economic and political efficiency. Granting this, the political efficiency gains that result from a constitutionally embedded generality standard need not be evaluated 'net of' economic efficiency losses. See § 8.1.
2. As has been suggested, even if one were to grant the existence of the efficiency frontier, the general theorem of second best 'shows the futility of "piecemeal welfare economics"' (Lipsey and Lancaster 1956, p. 17). See also § 5.2.
3. Of course, as has been repeatedly emphasized, the theory cannot, in fact, accommodate the moral force of rights. *Inter alia*, utilitarian considerations can always trump the rights which are 'justified' on utilitarian grounds. Granting this, the right-based rule of law

envisioned by social welfare theorists does not contemplate a correlative duty to respect the rights which they regard as instrumentally important.

4. What can be said is that the state may properly assume 'protective' and 'productive' roles. The former contemplates a state which 'emerges as the enforcing agency or institution ...charged with the single responsibility of enforcing agreed-on rights and claims along with contracts which involve voluntarily negotiated exchanges of such claims'. The latter refers to the 'agency through which individuals provide themselves with "public goods" in postconstitutional contract' (Buchanan [1975] 2000, pp. 88–89).
5. This formulation both acknowledges the subjectivity and mutability of individual preference and value structures and rejects the idea of a supraindividualistic public good. See, for example, Buchanan (1991, p. 16) and § 3.2.
6. Recall that the greatest possible equal liberty is to be promoted, and that the 'principle of equal liberty, when applied to the political procedure defined by the constitution' is referred to as 'the principle of (equal) participation' (Rawls 1971, p. 221).
7. See, for example, Nozick (1974), Kukathes and Pettit (1990, p. 31) and § 2.2.
8. As was suggested in § 9.8, a constitutional prohibition against 'bundling legislation' is a *sine qua non* for equal political participation. Insofar as omnibus appropriations, revenue and other bills are prohibited, 'logrolling' would be more difficult, and individual bills would have to be considered seriatim. This, it seems clear, would slow the legislative process and, *mutatis mutandis*, slow the growth of government.
9. See also §§ 4.4 and 5.2.

# References


Aaron, H.J. (1994), 'Public policy, values, and consequences', *Journal of Economic Perspectives*, **8**(2), 3–21.

Acemoglu, D. and T. Verdier (2000), 'The choice between market failures and corruption', *American Economic Review*, **90**(1), 194–211.

Almond, B. (1993), 'Rights', in Peter Singer (ed.), *A Companion to Ethics*, Cambridge, MA: Blackwell Publishers, Ltd., pp. 259–269.

Armey, Congressman Dick, 'How taxes corrupt', *The Wall Street Journal*, June 19, 1996.

Arrow, K.J. (1951), *Social Choice and Individual Value*, New Haven: Yale University Press.

Arrow, Kenneth J. (1969), 'The organization of economic activity: Issues pertinent to the choice of market versus non-market allocation', in *The Analysis and Evaluation of Public Expenditures: The PBB-System*, Joint Economic Committee, 91st Cong., 1st sess., vol. 1. Washington, DC: US Government Printing office.

Asea, P.K. (1996), 'The informal sector: Baby or bath water?', *Carnegie-Rochester Conference Series on Public Policy*, **45**, 163–171.

Bardhan, P. (1997), 'Corruption and development: A review of the issues', *Journal of Economic Literature*, **35**(3), 1320–1346.

Baron, J.N. and M.T. Hannan (1994), 'The impact of economics on contemporary sociology', *Journal of Economic Literature*, **32**(3), 1111–1146.

Barry, Brian (1989), *Theories of Justice*, Berkeley: University of California Press.

Becker, G.S. (1993), 'Nobel lecture: The economic way of looking at behavior', *Journal of Political Economy*, **101**(3), 385–409.

Black, Duncan (1958), *Theory of Committees and Elections*, Cambridge: Cambridge University Press.

Blaug, M. (2001), 'No history of ideas, please, we're economists', *Journal of Economic Perspectives*, **15**(1), 145–164

Bolton, G.E. and A. Ockenfels (2000), 'ERC: A theory of equity, reciprocity, and competition', *American Economic Review*, **90**(1), 166–193.

Bovard, James (1992), 'A Fruitless Massacre in California', *The Wall Street Journal*, August 11, 1992.

Bovard, James (1999), *Freedom in Chains: The Rise of the State and the Demise of the Citizen*, New York: St. Martin's Press.

Braguinsky, S. (1996), 'Corruption and Schumpeterian growth in different economic environments', *Contemporary Economic Policy*, **14**(3), 14–25.

Brennan, Geoffrey (1995), 'The contribution of economics', in Robert E. Goodin and Philip Pettit (eds), A *Companion to Contemporary Political Philosophy*, Cambridge, MA: Blackwell Publishers, Ltd., pp. 123–156.

Brennan, Geoffrey and James M. Buchanan (1985), *The Reason of Rules: Constitutional Political Economy*, reprinted in Geoffrey Brennan, Hartmut Kliemt and Robert D. Tollison (eds) (2000), *The Collected Works of James M. Buchanan*, vol. 10, Indianapolis: Liberty Fund.

Buchanan, J.M. (1954), 'Social choice, democracy, and free markets', *Journal of Political Economy*, 62, 114–123.

Buchanan, James M. (1959), 'Positive economics, welfare economics, and political economy', in Geoffrey Brennan, Hartmut Kliemt and Robert D. Tollison (eds) (1999), *The Collected Works of James M. Buchanan*, vol. I, Indianapolis: Liberty Fund, pp. 191–209.

Buchanan, James M. (1962), 'Politics, policy, and the Pigovian margins', in Geoffrey Brennan, Hartmut Kliemt and Robert D. Tollison (eds) (1999), *The Collected Works of James M. Buchanan*, vol. I, Indianapolis: Liberty Fund, pp. 60–74.

Buchanan, James M. (1967), *Public Finance in Democratic Process: Fiscal Institutions and Individual Choice*, reprinted in Geoffrey Brennan, Hartmut Kliemt and Robert D. Tollison (eds) (1999), *The Collected Works of James M. Buchanan*, vol. 4, Indianapolis: Liberty Fund.

Buchanan, James M. (1968), *The Demand and Supply of Public Goods*, reprinted in Geoffrey Brennan, Hartmut Kliemt and Robert D. Tollison (eds) (1999), *The Collected Works of James M. Buchanan*, vol. 5, Indianapolis: Liberty Fund.

Buchanan, James M. (1969), *Cost and Choice: An Inquiry in Economic Theory*, reprinted in Geoffrey Brennan, Hartmut Kliemt and Robert D. Tollison (eds) (1999), *The Collected Works of James M. Buchanan*, vol. 6, Indianapolis: Liberty Fund.

Buchanan, James M. (1975), *The Limits of Liberty: Between Anarchy and Leviathan*, reprinted in Geoffrey Brennan, Hartmut Kliemt and Robert D. Tollison (eds) (2000), *The Collected Works of James M. Buchanan*, vol. 7, Indianapolis: Liberty Fund.

Buchanan, James M. (1980), 'Rent seeking and profit seeking', in Geoffrey Brennan, Hartmut Kliemt and Robert D. Tollison (eds) (1999), *The Collected Works of James M. Buchanan*, vol. I, Indianapolis: Liberty Fund, pp. 103–115.

Buchanan, James M. (1989), 'The ethics of constitutional order', in Geoffrey

Brennan, Hartmut Kliemt and Robert D. Tollison (eds) (1999), *The Collected Works of James M. Buchanan*, vol. I, Indianapolis: Liberty Fund, pp. 368–373.

Buchanan, James M. (1990), 'Socialism is dead but Leviathan lives on', The John Bonython Lecture, CIS Occasional Paper 30, Sydney: Centre for Independent Studies, in Geoffrey Brennan, Hartmut Kliemt and Robert D. Tollison (eds) (1999), *The Collected Works of James M. Buchanan*, vol. I, Indianapolis: Liberty Fund, pp. 179–188.

Buchanan, James M. (1991), *The Economics and the Ethics of Constitutional Order*, Ann Arbor: The University of Michigan Press.

Buchanan, J.M. (1994a), 'Choosing what to choose', *Journal of Institutional and Theoretical Economics*, **150**(1), 123–135.

Buchanan, James M. (1994b), *Ethics and Economic Progress*, Norman: University of Oklahoma Press.

Buchanan, James M. and Roger D. Congleton (1998), *Politics by Principle not Interest: Towards Nondiscriminatory Democracy*, Cambridge: Cambridge University Press.

Buchanan, James M. and Gordon Tullock (1962), *The Calculus of Consent: Logical Foundations of Constitutional Democracy*, Ann Arbor: University of Michigan Press.

Carey, J. and Irene M. Kunii (2001), 'Chips: Breaking the light barrier', *Business Week*, April 16, 74–75.

Carroll, C.D. (2000), 'Requiem for the representative consumer? Aggregate implications of microeconomic consumption behavior', *American Economic Association Papers and Proceedings*, **90**(2), 110–115.

Carroll, C.D., J. Overland and D.N. Weil (2000), 'Savings and growth with habit formation', *American Economic Review*, **90**(3), 341–355.

Cheung, S.N.S. (1996), 'A simplistic general equilibrium theory of corruption', *Contemporary Economic Policy*, **14**(3), 1–5.

Conlisk, J. (1996), 'Why bounded rationality?', *Journal of Economic Literature*, **34**(2), 669–700.

Council of Economic Advisers (1989), *Economic Report of the President*, Washington, D.C.: U.S. Government Printing Office.

Cox, J.C. and S. Epstein (1989), 'Preference reversals without the independence axiom', *American Economic Review*, **79**(3), 408–426.

Davis, N.A. (1993), 'Contemporary deontology', in Peter Singer (ed.), *A Companion to Ethics*, Cambridge, MA: Blackwell Publishers, Ltd., 205–218.

Demsetz, H. (1969), 'Information and efficiency: Another viewpoint', *Journal of Law and Economics*, **12**(1), 1–22.

Demsetz, H. (1996), 'The primacy of economics: An explanation of the

comparative success of economics in the social sciences', *Economic Inquiry*, **35**(1), 1–11.
Dixit, Avinash (1996), *The Making of Economic Policy: A Transaction Cost Politics Perspective*, Cambridge: Cambridge University Press.
Dowell, R.S., R.S. Goldfarb and W.B. Griffith (1998), 'Economic man as a moral individual', *Economic Inquiry*, **36**(4), 645–653.
Duffie, D. and H. Sonnenschein (1989), 'Arrow and general equilibrium theory', *Journal of Economic Literature*, **27**(2), 565–598.
Dworkin, Ronald (1978), *Taking Rights Seriously*, Cambridge, MA: Harvard University Press.
Elster, J. (1989), 'Social norms and economic theory', *Journal of Economic Perspectives*, **3**(4), 99–117.
Epstein, R. (1992), 'Property rights and environmental protection', *Cato Policy Report*, 14.
Fehr, E. and S. Gächter (2000), 'Fairness and retaliation: The economics of reciprocity', *Journal of Economic Perspectives*, **14**(3), 159–181.
Felton, E. (1994), 'Feeding frenzy at the public trough', *Washington Times*, November 18.
Foster, J. (2000), 'Is there a role for transaction cost economics if we view firms as complex adaptive systems?', *Contemporary Economic Policy*, **18**(4), 369–385.
Frank, R.H. (1996), 'The political economy of preference falsification: Timur Kuran's "Private truths, public lies"', *Journal of Economic Literature*, **34**(1), 115–123.
Friedman, Milton (1953), *Essays in Positive Economics*, Chicago and London: The University of Chicago Press.
Fuhrer, J.C. (2000), 'Habit formation in consumption and its implications for monetary-policy models', *American Economic Review*, **90**(3), 367–390.
Fuller, Lon L. (1971), *The Morality of Law*, New Haven, Connecticut: Yale University Press.
Furubotn, E.G. (1964), 'Investment alternatives and the supply schedule of the firm', *Southern Economic Journal*, **31**(1), 21–37.
Furubotn, E.G. (1965), 'The orthodox production function and the adaptability of capital', *Western Economic Journal*, **3**(3), 288–300.
Furubotn, E.G. (1970), 'Long-run analysis and the form of the production function', *Economia Internazionale*, **23**(1), 3–35.
Furubotn, E.G. (1971), 'Economic organization and welfare distribution', *The Swedish Journal of Economics*, **73**(4), 409–416.
Furubotn, E.G. (1991), 'General equilibrium models, transaction costs, and the concept of efficient allocation in a capitalist economy', *Journal of Institutional and Theoretical Economics*, **147**(4), 662–686.
Furubotn, Eirik G. (1994), *Future Development of the New Institutional*

*Economics: Extension of the Neoclassical Model or New Construct?*, Jena: Max-Planck Institute for Research into Economic Systems.

Furubotn, E.G. (1999), 'Economic efficiency in a world of frictions', *Journal of Law and Economics*, **8**, 179–197.

Furubotn, Eirik G. and Svetozar Pejovich (1974), *The Economics of Property Rights*, Cambridge, MA: Ballinger.

Furubotn, Eirik G. and Rudolf Richter (1991), *The New Institutional Economics*, Tübingen: J.C.B. Mohr.

Furubotn, Eirik G. and Rudolf Richter (1997), *Institutions and Economic Theory: The Contribution of the New Institutional Economics*, Ann Arbor: The University of Michigan Press.

Garoupa, N. (2000), 'The economics of organized crime and optimal law enforcement', *Economic Inquiry*, **38**(2), 278–288.

Gauthier, David (1986), *Morals by Agreement*, Oxford: Oxford University Press.

Goldberg, P.K. and G. Maggi (1999), 'Protection for sale: An empirical investigation', *American Economic Review*, **89**(5), 1135–1155.

Goodin, R.E. (1993), 'Utility and the good', in Peter Singer (ed.), *A Companion to Ethics*, Cambridge, MA: Blackwell Publishers, Ltd., pp. 241–248.

Gort, M. and R. Boddy (1965), 'Vintage effects and the time path of investment in production relations', mimeographed, Conference on Research in Income and Wealth, New York, National Bureau of Economic Research.

Graaff, J. de V. (1957), *Theoretical Welfare Economics*, Cambridge: Cambridge University Press.

Grossman, G. and E. Helpman (1994), 'Protection for sale', *American Economic Review*, **84**(4), 833–850.

Gutfeld, R. (1990), 'Pure Plays', *The Wall Street Journal*, October 29.

Haavelmo, T. (1997), 'Econometrics and the welfare state', *American Economic Review*, **87**(6), 13–15.

Hahn, Frank (1982), 'On some difficulties of the utilitarian economist', in A. Sen and B. Williams (eds), *Utilitarianism and Beyond*, Cambridge: Cambridge University Press, pp. 187–198.

Hahn, R.W. (1998), 'Government analysis of the benefits and costs of regulation', *Journal of Economic Perspectives*, **12**(4), 201–210.

Hampton, Jean (1995), 'Contract and consent', in Robert E. Goodin and Philip Pettit (eds), *A Companion to Contemporary Political Philosophy*, Cambridge, MA: Blackwell Publishers, Ltd., pp. 379–393.

Harbough, W.T. and K. Krause (2000), 'Children's altruism in public good and dictator experiments', *Economic Inquiry*, **38**(1), 95–109.

Hausman, D.M. and M.S. McPherson (1993), 'Taking ethics seriously: Economics and contemporary moral philosophy', *Journal of Economic Literature*, **31**(2), 671–731.

Hausman, D.M. and M.S. McPherson (1996), *Economic Analysis and Moral Philosophy*, Cambridge: Cambridge University Press.

Hayek, Friedrick A. (1948), 'The use of knowledge in society', in *Individualism and Economic Order*, Chicago: University of Chicago Press, pp. 77–91.

Heiner, R.A. (1983), 'The origin of predictable behavior', *American Economic Review*, **73**(4), 560–595.

Henrich, J. (2000), 'Does culture matter in economic behavior? Ultimatum game bargaining among the machiguena of the Peruvian Amazon', *American Economic Review*, **90**(4), 973–979.

Hicks, J.R. (1939), *Value and Capital: An Inquiry into Some Fundamental Principles of Economic Theory*, Oxford: The Clarendon Press.

Howe, R.E. and J.E. Roemer (1981), 'Rawlsian justice as the core of a game', *American Economic Review*, **71**(5), 880–895.

Jordan, J. (2001), 'Hayekian economic infrastructure as a foundation for sustained prosperity', *Contemporary Economic Policy*, **19**(1), 20–26.

Kant, I. (1785), *Fundamental Principles of the Metaphysic of Morals*, translated by T.K. Abbott (1988): Prometheus Books.

Keita, L.D. (1992), *Science, Rationality, and Neoclassical Economics*, Newark: University of Delaware Press.

Klamer, A. (1989), 'A conversation with Amartya Sen', *Journal of Economic Perspectives*, **3**(1), 135–150.

Knox, T.M. (1999), 'The volunteer's folly and socio-economic man: Some thoughts on altruism, rationality, and community', *The Journal of Socio-Economics*, **28**(4), 475–492.

Krug, B. (1999), 'On custom in economics: The case of humanism and trade regimes', *Journal of Institutional and Theoretical Economics*, **155**(3), 405–428.

Kukathes, Chandran and Philip Pettit (1990), *Rawls: A Theory of Justice and Its Critics*, Stanford: Stanford University Press.

Kuran, Timur (1991), 'Cognitive limitations and preference evolution', *Journal of Institutional and Theoretical Economics*, **147**(2), 241–273.

Kymlicka, W. (1993), 'The social contract tradition', in Peter Singer (ed.), *A Companion to Ethics*, Cambridge, MA: Blackwell Publishers, Ltd., pp. 186–196.

Leibenstein, H. (1985), 'On relaxing the maximization postulate', *Journal of Behavioral Economics*, **14**, 5–19.

Lewin, S.B. (1996), 'Economics and psychology: Lessons for our own day from the early twentieth century', *Journal of Economic Literature*, **34**(3), 1293–1323.

Lipsey, R. and K. Lancaster (1956), 'The general theory of second best', *Review of Economic Studies*, **24**(63), 11–32.

Lizzeri, A. and N. Persico (2001), 'The provision of public goods under alternative electoral incentives', *American Economic Review*, **91**(1), 225–239.

Lui, F.T. (1996), 'Three aspects of corruption', *Contemporary Economic Policy*, **14**(3), 26–29.

Luzzati, T. (1999), 'A piece of evidence regarding the full rationality of economic agents', *Journal of Institutional and Theoretical Economics*, **155**(3), 567–572.

Lyons, David (1982), 'Utility and rights', in Jeremy Waldron (ed.), *Theories of Rights*, New York: Oxford University Press, Inc.

Mansfield, Edwin and Gary Yohe (2000), *Microeconomics, Tenth Edition*, New York: W.W. Norton & Company, Inc.

Manski, C.F. (2000), 'Economic analysis of social interactions', *Journal* of Economic Perspectives, **14**(3), 115–136.

Mauro, P. (1995), 'Corruption and growth', *Quarterly Journal of Economics*, **110**(3), 681–712.

Melitz, J. (1965), 'Friedman and Machlup on the significance of testing economic assumptions', *Journal of Political Economy*, **73**(1), 37–60.

Miller, G.J. (1997), 'The impact of economics on contemporary political science', *Journal of Economic Literature*, **35**(3), 1173–1204.

Mitra, D. (1999), 'Endogenous lobby formation and endogenous protection: A long-run model of trade policy determination', *American Economic Review*, **89**(5), 1116–1134.

Mixon, F.G., Jr. and D.L. Hobson (2001), 'Intergovernmental grants and the positioning of presidential primaries and caucuses: Empirical evidence from the 1992, 1996 and 2000 election cycles', *Contemporary Economic Policy*, **19**(1), 27–38.

Muller, Jerry Z. (1993), *Adam Smith in His Time and Ours: Designing the Decent Society*, Princeton, NJ: Princeton University Press.

Myerson, R. (1999), 'Nash equilibrium and the history of economic theory', *Journal of Economic Literature*, **37**(3), 1067–1082.

Nelson, J.A. (1995), 'Feminism and economics', *Journal of Economic Perspectives*, **9**(2), 131–148.

North, D.C. (1994), 'Economic performance through time', *American Economic Review*, **84**(3), 359–368.

Novshek, W. and H. Sonnenschein (1987), 'General equilibrium with free entry: A synthetic approach to the theory of perfect competition', *Journal of Economic Literature*, **25**(3), 1281–1306.

Nozick, Robert (1974), *Anarchy, State and Utopia*, New York: Basic Books, Inc., Publishers.

Office of Management and Budget (2001), *Analytical Perspectives*, Budget of the United States Government, Fiscal Year 2002, Washington, DC: US Government Printing Office.

Office of Management and Budget (2001), *Budget*, Budget of the United States Government, Fiscal Year 2002, Washington, DC: US Government Printing Office.

Office of Management and Budget (2001), *A Citizen's Guide to the Federal Budget*, Budget of the United States Government, Fiscal Year 2002, Washington, DC: US Government Printing Office.

Office of Management and Budget (2001), *Historical Tables*, Budget of the United States Government, Fiscal Year 2002, Washington, DC: US Government Printing Office.

O'Neill, O. (1993), 'Kantian ethics', in Peter Singer (ed.), *A Companion to Ethics*, Cambridge, MA: Blackwell Publishers, Ltd., pp. 175–185.

Ornstein, Norman J., Thomas E. Mann and Michael I. Malbin (2000), *Vital Statistics on Congress, 1999–2000*, Washington, DC: The AEI Press.

Ostrom, E. (2000), 'Collective action and the evolution of social norms', *Journal of Economic Perspectives*, **14**(3), 137–158.

Paton, H.J. (1964), *Immanuel Kant Groundwork of the Metaphysic of Morals*, New York: Harper Torchbooks.

Peletier, B.D., R.A.J. Dur and O.H. Swank (1999), 'Voting on the budget deficit: Comment', *American Economic Review*, **89**(5), 1377–1381.

Persky, J. (1995), 'Retrospective: The ethology of *homo economicus*', *Journal of Economic Perspectives*, **19**(2), 221–231.

Pettit, P. (1993), 'Consequentialism', in Peter Singer (ed.), *A Companion to Ethics*, Cambridge, MA: Blackwell Publishers, Ltd., pp. 230–240.

Pindyck, Robert S. and Daniel L. Rubinfeld (1997), *Microeconomics, Fourth Edition*, Upper Saddle River, New Jersey: Prentice Hall.

Pingle, M. (1992), 'Costly optimization: An experiment', *Journal of Economic Behavior and Organization*, **17**(1), 3–30.

Pollak, R.A. (1985), 'A transaction cost approach to families and households', *Journal of Economic Literature*, **13**(2), 581–608.

Posner, R.A. (1975), 'The economic approach to law', *Texas Law Review*, **53**, 757–782.

Posner, Richard A. (1999), *The Problematics of Moral and Legal Theory*, Cambridge, MA: Harvard University Press.

Prybyla, J.S. (1995), 'Modernization and modernity in the process of economic growth', *Issues and Studies*, **31**(4), 1–27.

Rabin, M. and R.H. Thaler (2001), 'Risk aversion', *Journal of Economic Perspectives*, **15**(1), 219–232.

Rawls, John (1971), *A Theory of Justice*, Cambridge, MA: The Belknap Press of Harvard University Press.

Rawls, John (1989), 'Themes in Kant's moral philosophy', in Samuel Freeman (ed.) (1999), *John Rawls: Collected Papers*, Cambridge, MA and London, England: Harvard University Press, pp. 497–528.

Rawls, John (1996), *Political Liberalism*, New York: Columbia University Press.

Robinson, Joan (1962), *Economic Philosophy*, London: C.A. Watts & Co.

Robson, A.J. (2001), 'The biological basis of economic behavior', *Journal of Economic Literature*, **39**(1), 11–33.

Rosen, Harvey S. (1999), *Public Finance, Fifth Edition*, Boston, MA: Irwin McGraw Hill.

Roth, T.P. (1972), 'The subjective production function: An approach to its determination', *The Engineering Economist*, **17**(4), 249–259.

Roth, T.P. (1974), 'The demand for a single variable productive service and the adaptability of capital', *Artha Vijnana*, **15**(4), 421–431.

Roth, T.P. (1975), 'The multi-equation utility function, information, and the optimal commodity bundle', *Metroeconomica*, **27**(2–3), 137–149.

Roth, T.P. (1977), 'Imperfect knowledge and the problem of choice among alternative production techniques', *The Engineering Economist*, **22**(4), 277–297.

Roth, T.P. (1979), 'Empirical cost curves and the production-theoretic short-run: A reconciliation', *Quarterly Review of Economics and Business*, **19**(3), 35–47.

Roth, T.P. (1995), 'Predation, cost-based tests and predatory intent, *Journal of Legal Economics*, **5**(1), 35–47.

Roth, Timothy (1998), *The Present State of Consumer Theory: The Implications for Social Welfare Theory*, Lanham, MD, New York and Oxford: University Press of America.

Roth, Timothy (1999), *Ethics, Economics and Freedom: The Failure of Consequentialist Social Welfare Theory*, Aldershot, UK and Brookfield, US: Ashgate.

Saint-Paul, G. (2000), 'The "new political economy": Recent books by Allen Drazen and Torsten Persson and Guido Tabellini', *Journal of Economic Literature*, **38**(4), 915–925.

Salanié, Bernard (2000), *The Microeconomics of Market Failures*, Cambridge, MA and London, England: The MIT Press.

Sandmo, A. (1990), 'Buchanan on political economy: A review article', *Journal of Economic Literature*, **28**(1), 50–65.

Schneider, F. and D.H. Enste (2000), 'Shadow economies: Size, causes, and consequences', *Journal of Economic Literature*, **38**(1), 77–114.

Scruton, Roger (1994), *Modern Philosophy: An Introduction and Survey*, New York: Penguin Books.

Sen, A. (1979), 'The welfare basis of real income comparisons: A survey', *Journal of Economic Literature*, **17**(1), 1–45.

Sen, Amartya (1992), *Inequality, Reexamined*, Cambridge, MA: Harvard University Press.

Sen, A. (1995), 'Rationality and social choice', *American Economic Review*, **85**(1), 1–24.

Simon, Herbert (1992), 'Introductory comment', in Massimo Egidi, Robin Marris and Riccardo Viale (eds), *Economics, Bounded Rationality and the Cognitive Revolution*, Aldershot, UK and Brookfield, US: Edward Elgar, pp. 3–7.

Slesnick, D. (1998), 'Empirical approaches to the measurement of welfare', *Journal of Economic Literature*, **36**(4), 2108–2165.

Smith, Adam (1759), *The Theory of Moral Sentiments*, reprinted in D.D. Raphael and A.L. Macfie (eds) (1976), Oxford: Oxford University Press.

Smith, Adam (1776), *An Inquiry into the Nature and Causes of the Wealth of Nations*, reprinted in W.B. Todd (ed.) (1976), Glasgow Edition of *The Works and Correspondence of Adam Smith*, vol. I, Oxford: Oxford University Press.

Starmer, C. (2000), 'Developments in non-expected utility theory: The hunt for a descriptive theory of choice under risk', *Journal of Economic Literature*, **38**(2), 332–382.

Stigler, George (1987), *The Theory of Price*, New York: Macmillan Publishing Company.

Stigler, G. and G.S. Becker (1977), 'De gustibus non est disputandum', *American Economic Review*, **67**(2), 76–90.

Stiglitz, Joseph (1988), *Economics of the Public Sector*, New York: W.W. Norton & Company.

Stiglitz, J. (1998), 'The private uses of public interests: Incentives and institutions', *Journal of Economic Perspectives*, **12**(2), 3–22.

Sugden, R. (1993), 'Welfare, resources and capabilities: A review of *Inequality Reexamined* by Amartya Sen', *Journal of Economic Literature*, **31**(4), 1947–1962.

Ten, C.L. (1995), 'Constitutionalism and the rule of law', in Robert E. Goodin and Philip Pettit (eds), *A Companion to Contemporary Political Philosophy*, Cambridge, MA: Blackwell Publishers Ltd., pp. 394–403.

Thaler, R.H. (2000), 'From homo economicus to homo sapiens', *Journal of Economic Perspectives*, **14**(1), 133–141.

Tribe, K. (1999), 'Adam Smith: Critical theorist', *Journal of Economic Literature*, **37**(2), 609–632.

Tullock, G. (1996), 'Corruption theory and practice', *Contemporary Economic Policy*, **14**(3), 6–13.

Tversky, A. and R.H. Thaler (1990), 'Preference reversals', *Journal of Economic Perspectives*, **4**(2), 201–211.

US Congress Joint Economic Committee (1979), *The 1979 Joint Economic Report*, Washington, DC: US Government Printing Office.

United States Senate, Committee on the Judiciary (1981), *Balanced Budget-*

*Tax Limitation Constitutional Amendment*, Washington, DC: US Government Printing Office.

Viscusi, W. Kip, John M. Vernon and Joseph E. Harrington (2000), *Economics of Regulation and Antitrust*, Cambridge, MA and London, England: The MIT Press.

Waldron, Jeremy (1995), *Theories of Rights*, Oxford: Oxford University Press.

Wallis, J.J. (2000), 'American government finance in the long run: 1790 to 1990', *Journal of Economic Perspectives*, **14**(1), 61–82.

Warke, T. (2000), 'Classical utilitarianism and the methodology of determinate choice, in economics and ethics', *Journal of Economic Methodology*, **7**(3), 373–394.

Weingast, B.R. (1991), 'The political institutions of representative government: Legislatures', in Eirik G. Furubotn and Rudolf Richter (eds), *The New Institutional Economics*, Tübingen: J.C.B. Mohr (Paul Siebeck).

Wilde, K.D., A.D. LeBaron and D. Israelsen (1985), 'Knowledge, uncertainty and behavior', *American Economic Association Papers and Proceedings*, **75**(2), 403–408.

Williamson, Oliver E. (1985), *The Economic Institutions of Capitalism*, New York: The Free Press.

Wong, S. (1973), 'The "F-twist" and the methodology of Paul Samuelson', *American Economic Review*, **63**(3), 312–325.

# Index